First World War
and Army of Occupation
War Diary
France, Belgium and Germany

8 DIVISION
24 Infantry Brigade,
Brigade Machine Gun Company
24 January 1916 - 30 June 1916

WO95/1723/2

The Naval & Military Press Ltd
www.nmarchive.com
Published in association with The National Archives

Published by

The Naval & Military Press Ltd

Unit 10 Ridgewood Industrial Park,

Uckfield, East Sussex,

TN22 5QE England

Tel: +44 (0) 1825 749494

www.naval-military-press.com

www.nmarchive.com

This diary has been reprinted in facsimile from the original. Any imperfections are inevitably reproduced and the quality may fall short of modern type and cartographic standards.

© Crown Copyright
Images reproduced by permission of The National Archives, London, England, 2015.

Contents

Document type	Place/Title	Date From	Date To
Heading	8th Division 24th Infy Bde 24th Machine Gun Coy Jan 1916 1918 Feb		
Heading	War Diary 24th Machine Gun Company July 1916 24th Inf. Bde. 8th Div. Brigade Rejoined 8th Div. From 23rd Div. III Corps. 15.7.16		
Miscellaneous	To:- D.A.G. 3rd Echelon	07/08/1916	07/08/1916
War Diary	Rainneville	01/07/1916	01/07/1916
War Diary	Henencourt	02/07/1916	03/07/1916
War Diary	Dernancourt	04/07/1916	06/07/1916
War Diary	Fricourt	07/07/1916	10/07/1916
War Diary	Bresle	11/07/1916	12/07/1916
War Diary	Molliens Au Bois	13/07/1916	13/07/1916
War Diary	Pierregot	14/07/1916	14/07/1916
War Diary	Poulainville	15/07/1916	15/07/1916
War Diary	Labeuvriere	16/07/1916	22/07/1916
War Diary	Beuvry	23/07/1916	31/07/1916
Heading	8th Division 24th Brigade 24th Machine Gun Co. August 1916		
Miscellaneous	D.A.G. Base	02/09/1916	02/09/1916
Heading	War Diary of 24th Machine Gun Company For The Month Of August 1916 Vol 8		
War Diary	Beuvry	01/08/1916	07/08/1916
War Diary	Vermelles	08/08/1916	14/08/1916
War Diary	Fouquereuil	15/08/1916	22/08/1916
War Diary	Vermelles	23/08/1916	31/08/1916
Heading	8th Division 24th Brigade 24th Machine Gun Co. September 1916		
Heading	War Diary By Captain F.E.C. Lewis For The Month Of September 1916 24 M G Coy Vol 9		
War Diary	Vermelles	01/09/1916	08/09/1916
War Diary	Fouquereuil	08/09/1916	16/09/1916
War Diary	Vermelles	17/09/1916	30/09/1916
Heading	8th Division 24th Brigade 24th Machine Gun Co. October 1916		
Heading	War Diary of the 24th M.G. Company For The Month Of October 1916 Vol 10		
War Diary	Vermelles	01/10/1916	10/10/1916
War Diary	Fouquereuil	11/10/1916	14/10/1916
War Diary	Hocquincourt	15/10/1916	16/10/1916
War Diary	Meaulte	17/10/1916	19/10/1916
War Diary	Delville Wood	20/10/1916	31/10/1916
Heading	8th Division 24th Brigade 24th Machine Gun Co. November 1916		
Miscellaneous	D.A.G. Base	03/12/1916	03/12/1916
Heading	War Diary of the 24th Machine Gun Company By Captain F.E.C. Lewis For The Month Of November 1916		
War Diary	Trones Wood	01/11/1916	01/11/1916
War Diary	Meaulte	02/11/1916	05/11/1916
War Diary	Carnoy	06/11/1916	06/11/1916

War Diary	Lesboeufs	07/11/1916	09/11/1916
War Diary	Carnoy	10/11/1916	13/11/1916
War Diary	Lesboeufs	14/11/1916	17/11/1916
War Diary	Carnoy	18/11/1916	18/11/1916
War Diary	Meaulte	19/11/1916	21/11/1916
War Diary	Fresneville	22/11/1916	30/11/1916
War Diary	Trones Wood	01/11/1916	01/11/1916
War Diary	Meaulte	02/11/1916	05/11/1916
War Diary	Carnoy	06/11/1916	06/11/1916
Heading	8th Division 24th Brigade 24th Machine Gun Co. December 1916		
Miscellaneous	D.A.G. Base	02/01/1917	02/01/1917
Heading	War Diary of the 24th Machine Gun Company For The Month Of December 1916 By Captain F.E.B. Lewis Vol 12		
War Diary	Fresneville	01/12/1916	30/12/1916
War Diary	Camp 16	31/12/1916	31/12/1916
Heading	War Diary of the 24th M.G. Coy For The Month Of January 1917 By Major F.E.B. Lewis Vol 13		
War Diary	Camp 16 Bronfay Farm	01/01/1917	10/01/1917
War Diary	Sailly-Le-Sec	11/01/1917	11/01/1917
War Diary	Epaumesnil	12/01/1917	22/01/1917
War Diary	Camp 12 Near Sailly Laurette	23/01/1917	25/01/1917
War Diary	Camp 17	26/01/1917	26/01/1917
War Diary	Trenches	26/01/1917	31/01/1917
Heading	War Diary of 24th Machine Gun Company For February 1917 By Major F.E.B. Lewis Vol 14		
Miscellaneous	D.A.G. Base	02/03/1917	02/03/1917
War Diary	Trenches	01/02/1917	09/02/1917
War Diary	Trenches (Bouchavesnes)	10/02/1917	10/02/1917
War Diary	Camp 117 Camp 12	11/02/1917	11/02/1917
War Diary	Camp 12 (Nr Chipilly)	12/02/1917	20/02/1917
War Diary	Camp 12 Suzanne	21/02/1917	21/02/1917
War Diary	Suzanne Camp 17	22/02/1917	22/02/1917
War Diary	Camp 17	23/02/1917	23/02/1917
War Diary	Camp 17 in Suzanne & Langton Brks	24/02/1917	28/02/1917
Heading	War Diary of 24th Machine Gun Company By Major F.E.B. Lewis For The Month Of March 1917 Vol 15		
War Diary	Camp 17 (Nr Suzanne) Langton Barracks (Nr Bouchavesnes)	01/03/1917	01/03/1917
War Diary	Langton Barracks	02/03/1917	06/03/1917
War Diary	Trenches	06/03/1917	08/03/1917
War Diary	Trenches (Lazarus)	08/03/1917	08/03/1917
War Diary	Trenches	09/03/1917	12/03/1917
War Diary	Trenches (Langton Brks)	13/03/1917	18/03/1917
War Diary	Trenches	19/03/1917	23/03/1917
War Diary	(Marriere Wood) Trenches	24/03/1917	24/03/1917
War Diary	Moislains (Billets)	25/03/1917	29/03/1917
War Diary	Moislains	30/03/1917	31/03/1917
Miscellaneous	O.C. 24th M.G. Coy	01/05/1917	01/05/1917
War Diary	Lieramont	01/04/1917	05/04/1917
War Diary	Heudicourt	06/04/1917	15/04/1917
War Diary	Nurlu	15/04/1917	18/04/1917
War Diary	Lieramont	19/04/1917	23/04/1917
War Diary	Chapel Crossing	23/04/1917	26/04/1917
War Diary	Villers Guislains	27/04/1917	30/04/1917

Type	Description	Start	End
Heading	War Diary of the 24th Machine Gun Company For The Month Of May 1917 By Major E.C. Lewis Vol 17		
War Diary	Villers Guislains	01/05/1917	09/05/1917
War Diary	Lieramont	09/05/1917	11/05/1917
War Diary	Moislains	12/05/1917	29/05/1917
War Diary	Campi Nr Suzanne	29/05/1917	31/05/1917
War Diary	Sailly Laurette	31/05/1917	31/05/1917
Heading	War Diary of the 24th Machine Gun Company For The Month Of June 1917 By Captain G.M. Pratt Vol. 18		
War Diary	Sailly-Laurette	01/06/1917	01/06/1917
War Diary	Corbie	01/06/1917	03/06/1917
War Diary	Merris	03/06/1917	11/06/1917
War Diary	Sylvester Capel	11/06/1917	12/06/1917
War Diary	Belgium Scottish Camp	12/06/1917	14/06/1917
War Diary	Ypres (Line)	14/06/1917	14/06/1917
War Diary	Hooge Sector	15/06/1917	17/06/1917
War Diary	Ypres	18/06/1917	18/06/1917
War Diary	Trenches	18/06/1917	18/06/1917
War Diary	Hooge Sector	18/06/1917	18/06/1917
War Diary	Halifax Camp Nr Vlamertinghe	19/06/1917	20/06/1917
War Diary	Halifax Camp	20/06/1917	29/06/1917
War Diary	Ypres	29/06/1917	29/06/1917
War Diary	Trenches	29/06/1917	30/06/1917
Heading	War Diary of the 24th M.G. Company For The Month Of July 1917 By Lieut F.D. Beechman Vol 19		
War Diary	Ypres	01/07/1917	06/07/1917
War Diary	Montreal Camp	06/07/1917	08/07/1917
War Diary	Petigny	08/07/1917	21/07/1917
War Diary	Lespresses	21/07/1917	22/07/1917
War Diary	Bussebom	22/07/1917	23/07/1917
War Diary	Ypres	23/07/1917	23/07/1917
War Diary	Ypres Wreckerage	24/07/1917	26/07/1917
War Diary	Halfway House	26/07/1917	26/07/1917
War Diary	Ypres Wreckerage & Halfway House	26/07/1917	31/07/1917
War Diary	Ypres Wreckerage & Halfway House	29/07/1917	31/07/1917
War Diary	Hooge	31/07/1917	31/07/1917
War Diary	James Tr Chateau Wood	31/07/1917	31/07/1917
War Diary	Chateau Wood	31/07/1917	31/07/1917
War Diary	War Diary of the 24th Machine Gun Company For The Month Of August 1917 By Lieut G.U. Sully For Officer Commanding Vol 20		
Miscellaneous	B.B. 24th M.G. Company	31/08/1917	31/08/1917
War Diary	James Trench (Chateau Wood)	01/08/1917	01/08/1917
War Diary	Montreal Camp	02/08/1917	03/08/1917
War Diary	(Le Temple Near) Steenvoorde	04/08/1917	13/08/1917
War Diary	Halifax Camp	14/08/1917	15/08/1917
War Diary	Red Lodge (Westhoek)	15/08/1917	18/08/1917
War Diary	Swan Chateau	18/08/1917	18/08/1917
War Diary	Halifax Camp	19/08/1917	20/08/1917
War Diary	La Briarde (Caestre Area B)	20/08/1917	27/08/1917
War Diary	St. Yves (Ploegsteert Wd)	27/08/1917	28/08/1917
War Diary	Ploegsteert Wd	28/08/1917	31/08/1917
Miscellaneous	O.C. 24th Machine Gun Company	22/08/1917	22/08/1917
Miscellaneous	2 Div Signals Aldershot	26/10/1917	26/10/1917
Map	Map		
Map	Disposition Of Guns 1/Nzm-G Coy.		

Miscellaneous	Received From Local R.H. Neale	27/10/1937	27/10/1937
Heading	War Diary 24th Machine Gun Company For The Month Of September 1917		
War Diary	Leinster Rd Neuve Eglise T. 21 B. 15. Y 5	01/09/1917	17/09/1917
War Diary	Vickers Lines Le Romarin B 4 C 50.98	18/09/1917	30/09/1917
Heading	24th Machine Gun Company War Diary for The Month of October 1917		
War Diary	Vickers lines & Warneton Sector	01/10/1917	03/10/1917
War Diary	Larks Camp B 8 C 2 0 & Warneton sector	04/10/1917	31/10/1917
Heading	War Diary of the 24th Machine Gun Company Captain A.M. Pratt For The Month Of November 1917 Vol 23		
War Diary	Warneton Sector & Larks Camp B 8 C 2 0	01/11/1917	14/11/1917
War Diary	Sheet 36 F 26 C	15/11/1917	16/11/1917
War Diary	Ypres C 27 C	17/11/1917	18/11/1917
War Diary	St Jean C 27 C7.6	19/11/1917	20/11/1917
War Diary	Hop Factory Brandhoek H 8.A 50 85	21/11/1917	23/11/1917
War Diary	Passchendaele Sector & St Jean C 27 C 7 6	24/11/1917	30/11/1917
Heading	War Diary of the 24th Machine Gun Company For The Month Of December 1917 By Commanding 24th Machine Gun Company Vol 24		
Miscellaneous	24th Company Machine Gun Corps. Operation Order By Capt. A.M. Pratt	01/12/1917	01/12/1917
Miscellaneous	24th Company Machine Gun Corps Appendix to Operation Order		
Miscellaneous	Fire Orders		
Miscellaneous	Time Of Firing		
Miscellaneous	Programme Of Company Training		
Miscellaneous	24th Machine Gun Company Narrative Of The Operations	02/12/1917	02/12/1917
Miscellaneous	24th Company Machine Gun Corps Relief Orders By Captain A. Bennett	26/12/1917	26/12/1917
War Diary	D.5.D 70/20 (Sheet 27 NE)	01/12/1917	01/12/1917
War Diary	Paschendaele	02/12/1917	02/12/1917
War Diary	Wieltje	03/12/1917	03/12/1917
War Diary	Val-D'Acquin	04/12/1917	25/12/1917
War Diary	St Jean (Ypres)	25/12/1917	26/12/1917
War Diary	Barrage Posns Wolf Copse (N.W. of Passchendaele)	27/12/1917	31/12/1917
War Diary	Sheet 27 1/40000	01/02/1918	11/02/1918
Miscellaneous	Operation Orders By Capt Tonks O.C. B Coy	11/02/1918	11/02/1918
War Diary	28 Nei 1/10,000	12/02/1918	28/02/1918
Heading	23rd Division 24th Infy Bde 24th Machine Gun Coy Jan-Jun 1916		
Heading	War Diary of 24th Machine Gun Company For Months Of January February March 1916		
War Diary	B 26 A 7 1/2.6	24/01/1916	19/02/1916
War Diary	Vieux Berquin	20/02/1916	20/02/1916
War Diary	Labelle Hotesse	21/02/1916	21/02/1916
War Diary	I 3 B 5:7	22/02/1916	29/02/1916
War Diary	Bruay	01/03/1916	06/03/1916
War Diary	Grand Servins	07/03/1916	11/03/1916
War Diary	Ablain St Nazaire	12/03/1916	16/03/1916
War Diary	Ourton	17/03/1916	20/03/1916
War Diary	Hersin	21/03/1916	21/03/1916
War Diary	Aix Noulette	22/03/1916	31/03/1916
Heading	War Diary of 24th Inf Bde Machine Gun Company For Month Of April 1916 Vol IV		

War Diary	Aix-Noulette	01/04/1916	17/04/1916
War Diary	Hersin	18/04/1916	18/04/1916
War Diary	Bruay	19/04/1916	25/04/1916
War Diary	Sains-Les-Pernes	26/04/1916	26/04/1916
War Diary	Vincly	27/04/1916	30/04/1916
Heading	War Diary of 24th Brigade Machine Gun Company For Month Of May 1916 Vol 5		
War Diary	Vincly	01/05/1916	04/05/1916
War Diary	Palfart	05/05/1916	05/05/1916
War Diary	Hersin	06/05/1916	10/05/1916
War Diary	Aix Noulette	11/05/1916	16/05/1916
War Diary	Bouvigny Wood	17/05/1916	21/05/1916
War Diary	Bouvigny	22/05/1916	30/05/1916
War Diary	Fosse 10	31/05/1916	31/05/1916
Heading	War Diary of 24th Bde Machine Gun Company For June 1916 Vol 6		
War Diary	Fosse 10	01/06/1916	14/06/1916
War Diary	Pressy Les Pernes	15/06/1916	16/06/1916
War Diary	Groeuppe	17/06/1916	24/06/1916
War Diary	St. Saveur	25/06/1916	30/06/1916

8TH DIVISION
24TH INFY BDE

24TH MACHINE GUN COY.
~~JAN 1916-DEC 1917~~ 1918 FEB

24th Inf.Bde.
8th Div.

Brigade rejoined
8th Div. from 23rd
Div. III.Corps,
15.7.16.

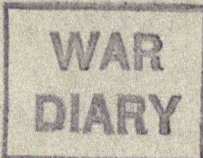

24th MACHINE GUN COMPANY.

J U L Y

1916

To:- D.A.G. 3rd Echelon

Herewith - Original War Diary of 94th
M G Coy.

P.C. Kevins
Captain
Comdg 94th M G Coy

7/8/16

Army Form C. 2118.

WAR DIARY
or
INTELLIGENCE SUMMARY
(Erase heading not required.)

Instructions regarding War Diaries and Intelligence Summaries are contained in F. S. Regs., Part II. and the Staff Manual respectively. Title Pages will be prepared in manuscript.

Place	Date	Hour	Summary of Events and Information	Remarks and references to Appendices
RAINNEVILLE	1/7/16	—	Company parade for semaphore practice in morning — Move at 9.0 P.M. to HÉNENCOURT WOOD	First.
HÉNENCOURT	2/7/16	—	Arrive HÉNENCOURT WOOD at 4.0 A.M., after much delay on road. Bivouack in westend of wood — ground and weather being dreadful.	R.e.
	3/7/16	—	At HÉNENCOURT WOOD. Company parade to fire on short range, and drill.	R.e.
DERNANCOURT	4/7/16	—	Move at 8.0 A.M. to DERNANCOURT. In afternoon Lt. Doman + Baller reconnoitre route to LA BOISELLE, and Lt. Perkins + Beecham route to FRICOURT. Heavy thunderstorm in afternoon. Coy. stood to in evening, in reduced kit, for night attack. Order to stand down arrived at 12.30 A.M.	R.e.
	5/7/16	—	At DERNANCOURT.	R.e.
	6/7/16	—	In morning Lt. Friend with 4. O.R. rode to MÉRICOURT to collect 4 remounts, and returned at 12.0 Noon with 2 chargers and 2 light draught horses. Lt. Perkins + Beecham reconnoitred ground between SHELTER WOOD and CONTALMAISON, returning 1.30 P.M. Coy. move at 4.0 P.M. to FRICOURT, stopping en route for tea at MÉAULTE. After tea No 3 section under Lt. Perkins joined 1st Worc. Regt. + moved with them to the DINGLE. No 2 section under Lt. Friend joined 2. E. Lancs. Regt. + moved with them to PATCH ALLEY. No 1 section under Lt. Doman moved independently to SHELTER WOOD. Feed and watered a section of 52 m. M.G.Coy.	

2449 Wt. W14957/M90 750,000 1/16 J.B.C. & A. Forms/C.2118/12.

WAR DIARY or INTELLIGENCE SUMMARY

Army Form C. 2118.

Place	Date	Hour	Summary of Events and Information	Remarks and references to Appendices
	6/7/16	—	Coy. H.Q. with No 4 Section under Lt. Dunlu, moved to LOVELY COPSE. Transport Lines in a field about ¾ mile S.W. of FRICOURT. All sections had letters at their positions by midnight.	A.e.
FRICOURT	7/7/16	—	Coy. R' Bde attach CONTALMAISON. No 3 Section moved at NOON to SHELTER WOOD there with Bn. H.Q. 1st Wilts Regt. on receipt of news that 2 Coys had entered the village, No 3 Section had orders to consolidate the village. Progress was slow owing to heavy rain, heavy shelling & the wounded head. No 3 Section had reached SHELTER ALLEY by 4.0 P.M. When retirement began, the attack having been unsupported. No 4 Section returned to their positions in SHELTER WOOD there by 6.0 P.M. They lost 1 killed and 5 wounded by shell fire. No 2 Section stayed in PATCH ALLEY. Lt. Friend going to SHELTER WOOD. Trench with Bn. H.Q. 2nd E. Lancs. Regt. to reconnoitre. Lt. Friend was there killed by H.E. shell. No 1 Section had orders to proceed to consolidate the CEMETERY, but as the attack failed, did not move. They bivouacked below into the enemy positions in CONTALMAISON during the day to support the attack. At 11.0 P.M. Lt. Donnan took 2 games of No 2 Section to SHELTER ALLEY to support 2 advanced Coys. of 1st Wilts Regt. During the day No 1 Section lost 5 wounded by shell fire. No 4 Section moved to SHELTER WOOD there at NOON, took up positions there. They lost 2 wounded by shell fire. Coy. H.Q. moved to trench near ROUND WOOD at NOON.	

2449 Wt. W14957/M90 750,000 1/16 J.B.C. & A. Forms/C.2118/12.

July 1st   Leave Raineville 9.0 PM (complete)
2nd   Arrive Hénencourt Wood 4.0 AM.
3rd   At Hénencourt Firing + grd drill
4th   ~~~~~~~~~~
4th   Move to Dernancourt 8.0 PM
5th   At Dernancourt   B+D to Bouzincourt / F+E to Fricourt
6th   Move to Fricourt 4.0 PM.
7th   1st attack on C.M.
8th   2nd "   "   "
9th   At Fricourt
10th   Leave Fricourt (supporting 39th Bde.)
11th   Arrive Bresle 5.30 AM.
12th   Move to Molliens au Bois 6.30 PM
13th   Move to Pierregot 2.15 PM
14th   Move to Pouleinville

WAR DIARY
or
INTELLIGENCE SUMMARY

Army Form C. 2118.

Place	Date	Hour	Summary of Events and Information	Remarks and references to Appendices
FRICOURT	7/7/16	—	At 10.0 P.M. No 2 Section now under Lt. Hicks came up & relieved No 3 Section in SHELTER WOOD Trench; No 3 Section returned to PATCH ALLEY between guns. Rain fell heavily through the afternoon & night, & the enemy continually shelled SHELTER WOOD Trench, BEECH TREE WOOD, ROUND WOOD, and SUNKEN ROAD.	S.C.
"	8/7/16	—	In morning, Coy. H.Q. moved back to LOZENGE WOOD. In afternoon, 7th Bde. was ordered to attack CONTALMAISON again, the village having been reported evacuated. No 3 Section moved up SUNKEN ROAD in rear of 2 reserve Coys of 1st W. Yorks. Regt. The attack did not develop, the village actually being very strongly held, and SHELTER WOOD Trench & SUNKEN ROAD being heavily barraged by enemy. No 3 & No 2 Sections each had 1 man wounded by shell fire. Meanwhile the 2 guns No 1 Section in SHELTER ALLEY had been in action against PEAKE WOOD which contained enemy machine guns. At 10.0 P.M. 3 guns of No 3 Section and 3 guns No 2 Section moved up to SHELTER ALLEY, taking up positions covering PEAKE WOOD and CONTALMAISON; the 2 guns under Lt. Dorman, and remaining 2 guns in SHELTER WOOD Trench, of No 1 Section returning to LOZENGE WOOD. During the day the weather improved, but the trenches were in a very bad state, with mud and water & casualties	S.C.

Place	Date	Hour	Summary of Events and Information	Remarks and references to Appendices
FRICOURT	9/7/16	—	No fresh developments during day. At 10.0 P.M. 2 guns No.1 Section relieved 2 guns No.4 Section in SHELTER WOOD, the latter moving to LOZENGE WOOD.	
"	10/7/16	—	O.C. received orders to place 2 guns in Pt.60 during the night, in order to support an attack on CONTALMAISON from the West by the 69 I.Bde. On the following afternoon O.C. Coy. reconnoitred the positions, and being unable exactly to locate Pt.60, gave Lt. Fletcher instructions to place 2 guns in position having the requisite field of fire — that is, positions enfilading the enemy trench which defended the West of CONTALMAISON, & covering the ground in rear of their trench. In morning 2 guns of No.1 Section opened fire on the enemy detraining from CONTALMAISON, towards MAMETZ WOOD. Several of the enemy were observed to fall. At 4.30 P.M. the 69 I.Bde. attacked the enemy across the West side of CONTALMAISON. 2 guns of No.2 Section under Lt. Hicks came into action at 5.5 P.M., enfilading the trench. Later a body of the enemy were seen retiring from the trench across Gunners CONTALMAISON; the above 2 guns opened fire on them at 650x, and accounted for about 30 or up to 50. In the morning, 3 men of No.2 Section manning a gun in SHELTER WOOD trench, were wounded by shell fire.	O.C.

Army Form C. 2118.

WAR DIARY
or
INTELLIGENCE SUMMARY

(Erase heading not required.)

Instructions regarding War Diaries and Intelligence Summaries are contained in F. S. Regs., Part II. and the Staff Manual respectively. Title Pages will be prepared in manuscript.

Place	Date	Hour	Summary of Events and Information	Remarks and references to Appendices
FRICOURT	10/7/16	–	At 8.30 P.M. the 1st M.G. Coy. arrived at SUNKEN ROAD to relieve the Coy. Relief complete by 12.45 A.M.	f.i.c
BRESLE	11/7/16	–	Sections on relief moved off independently with their transport. Sections billeted for an hour in a field near DERNANCOURT for tea; then proceeded to billets at BRESLE, the last section arriving at 5.0 A.M.	
	12/7/16	–	Roll Call in the morning showed that casualties (including sick) for the four days numbered 27. All guns etc. had been brought out on relief but to guns were out of action owing to shortage of men to man them. Cleaning up parades in morning. At 5.20 P.M. Coy moved to billets at Chateau.	f.i.c
MOLLIENS AU BOIS	13/7/16	–	At 2.0 P.M. Coy moved to billets in next village PIERREGOT. Billets neither 0 crowded. 2/Lt. Silly joined from GRANTHAM.	f.i.c
PIERREGOT	14/7/16	–	Cleaning up parades in morning. At 4.40 P.M. Coy moved to billets at POULAINVILLE. Men comfortable in large farm.	f.i.c
POULAINVILLE	15/7/16	–	At 4.30 A.M. Transport, with No 1 Section's load, under Lt. Dorman, move to LONGEAU to entrain.	f.i.c

Army Form C. 2118.

WAR DIARY
or
INTELLIGENCE SUMMARY
(Erase heading not required.)

Instructions regarding War Diaries and Intelligence Summaries are contained in F. S. Regs., Part II. and the Staff Manual respectively. Title Pages will be prepared in manuscript.

Place	Date	Hour	Summary of Events and Information	Remarks and references to Appendices
	15/7/16	—	Coy: fell in at 7.15 AM, reaching LONGUEAU Station at 9.45 AM. Train left LONGUEAU at 11.8 AM, and arrived BETHUNE at 6.0 P.M. Coy: marched off at 7.0 P.M. arriving at billets at LABEUVRIERE at 8.7 P.M. Billets good.	S.L.C.
LABEUVRIERE	16/7/16	—	Cleaning up parades.	S.L.C.
	17/7/16	—	10 O.R. Inspected & join the Coy. Transferred from 168th Trench Mortar Battery. Weather wet. In afternoon Coy moved to fresh billets about 1 mile on road to FOUQUEREUIL arriving at billets 5 P.M.	O.C.
	18/7/16	—	Firing on range + cleaning up in morning.	R.C.
	19/7/16	—	Parades for washing Rubber etc. in morning	R.C.
	20/7/16	—	The Brigade was inspected by G.O.C Army at HESDIGNE HESDIGNEUL at 2.0 P.M. 26 O.R. join the Coy, attached from the Bno. of the Bde.	R.C.
	21/7/16	—	2/Lt: Hutchins joins the Coy from GRANTHAM, with 10 O.R.	R.C.
	22/7/16	—	2/Lt: Hutchins goes to hospital with fractured Clavicle. In the morning the Coy moved to billets at BEUVRY. Billets good.	R.C.
BEUVRY	23/7/16	—	Church parade (C.& P.E.) in the morning	R.C.
	24/7/16	—	Half of the Coy parades for Baths. 15 O.R. join the Coy: from GRANTHAM. The following were awarded the Military Medal :— N° 195-74 Sgt R. Gooding. N° 19653 L/c T. Hind. N° 19587 Pte G. Earll	S.L.C.

Army Form C. 2118.

WAR DIARY
or
INTELLIGENCE SUMMARY
(Erase heading not required.)

Instructions regarding War Diaries and Intelligence Summaries are contained in F. S. Regs., Part II. and the Staff Manual respectively. Title Pages will be prepared in manuscript.

Place	Date	Hour	Summary of Events and Information	Remarks and references to Appendices
BEUVRY	25/7/16	—	Other half of the Coy. handed over to Battery. 2/Lt. A.R. Finn the Coy. from GRANTHAM.	S.L.C
	26/7/16	—	Officers i/c Sections reconnoitre trenches of CUINCHY Section. Weather very showery. Classes reopened for men requiring further M.G. instruction (chiefly new drafts.) There are 8 Classes with N.C.O. instructors.	S.L.C. S.L.C. S.L.C.
	27/7/16	—	O.C. Coy. & 2nd i/c Coy reconnoitre trenches of CUINCHY Section. Section Parades as usual. Lt. Higham joins the Coy, attached from 119th M.G. Coy.	
	28/7/16	—	Section parades as usual. Remaining Officers reconnoitre trenches of CUINCHY Section	
	29/7/16	—	2/Lt. Hides goes to hospital sick. In the evening guns & equipment of Nos 2, 3, 4 Sections moved to CAMBRIN and remain there during the night under a guard, preparatory to going to trenches on the following day.	
	30/7/16	—	At 10.0 P.M. Coy. receives "S.O.S. g 4.4" to stands to. "S.O.S Cancelled" received at 11.30 P.M. At 2.15 A.M. Coy. receives "S.O.S. A.28.1" & stands to. "S.O.S Cancelled" received at 3.30 AM. In the morning Lt. Dorman with 3 guns and 4-men teams, proceeds to take over the 3 left-hand positions of the CUINCHY Section from the 23rd M.G. Coy. While Lt. Fletcher with 4 guns, Lt. Perkins with 4 guns & Lt. Poulton with 5 guns; each with 4-men teams, take over the centre and right hand positions, picking up their guns at the dump at CAMBRIN on their way to trenches. All 16 guns in position, and relief complete by 11.15 AM. The remaining Officers and reserve teams of 4 men for each gun, remain in & billeted at BEUVRY.	S.L.C
	31/7/16	—	O.C. Coy. visits trenches. Reserve teams parade for semaphore practice etc.	S.L.C.

8th, Division.

24th, Brigade.

2 4th, Machine Gun Co.

August, 1916.

To D.A.G. BASE

Herewith War Diary for month of August 1916

S.L. Courtauld Lieut for Captain
Comdg 24th M G Coy

No. 24 MACHINE GUN COMPANY.
No. —
Date 2/9/16

WAR DIARY
OF
24TH MACHINE GUN COMPANY
FOR THE
MONTH OF
AUGUST 1916

Army Form C. 2118.

WAR DIARY
or
INTELLIGENCE SUMMARY
(Erase heading not required.)

Instructions regarding War Diaries and Intelligence Summaries are contained in F. S. Regs., Part II. and the Staff Manual respectively. Title Pages will be prepared in manuscript.

Place	Date	Hour	Summary of Events and Information	Remarks and references to Appendices
BEUVRY	1/8/16		Reserve teams parade for drill in morning. Overhead fire repeated on this & subsequent nights	V.L.C.
	2/8/16		Same as 1st.	d.c.c.
	3/8/16		2 O.R. of No. 3 Section wounded in trenches; one of these remained on duty. In morning, reserve teams relieved teams in trenches, and Lts. Tully, Higham, and Beecham relieved Lts. Dornan, Fletcher & Boulter	P.L.C. P.L.C.
	4/8/16		Reserve teams parade for drill etc	
	5/8/16		Company relieved in morning as follows:- No 1, 2 + 3 Sections by 141st M.G. Coy, and No. 4 Section by 97th M.G. Coy.	V.L.C.
	6/8/16		Section parades in morning for cleaning up etc. O.C. Coy. reconnoitred trenches of QUARRIES Sector.)	P.L.C.
	7/8/16		In afternoon, No 1 + 2 Sections, each with 8 guns relieved 10 guns of 141st M.G. Coy. in QUARRIES Sector. No. 1 Section under Lt. Dornan (C.y.) and Lt. Tully; to man positions in reserve line while No. 2 Section under Lt. Fletcher (C.y.) and Lt. Higham, took over positions in village line.	P.L.C.
VERMELLES	8/8/16		In afternoon Coy. Hdqs. and No. 3 + 4 Sections moved to cellars and dug outs in VERMELLES. Transport + P.M. Store moved to line at SAILLY LABOURSE. Exchange completed at 4 S.A.M. Capt. E. for 4 overhead waggons (for ammunition), and of the remaining Maxim guns of the Coy. for Vickers guns. One O.R. (No. 1 Section) wounded.	P.L.C.
	9/9/16		No. 3 + 4 Sections parade for cleaning out cellars etc. Overhead fire by adjacent units on "Tender Spots" behind enemy's line during this and subsequent nights. At midnight 23rd Bolm on left sent warning of expected enemy attack. However nothing happened.	P.L.C.
	10/8/16		4 O.R. Joined Coy. from G RANTHAM.	S.L.C.

2449 Wt. W14957/M90 750,000 1/16 J.B.C. & A. Forms/C.2118/12.

Army Form C. 2118.

WAR DIARY
or
INTELLIGENCE SUMMARY
(Erase heading not required.)

Instructions regarding War Diaries and Intelligence Summaries are contained in F. S. Regs, Part II. and the Staff Manual respectively. Title Pages will be prepared in manuscript.

Place	Date	Hour	Summary of Events and Information	Remarks and references to Appendices
VERMELLES	11/8/16	-	In afternoon No 3 & 4 Sections, under Lt. Perkins & Bowlin, relieved No 1 & 2 Sections, who returned EVERMELLES.	S.L.C.
	12/8/16	-	No 1 & 2 Sections paraded for gun cutting and braking bricks for transport.	S.L.C.
	13/8/16	-	Same as 12th. 1 O.R. rejoins from France	P.L.C.
	14/8/16	-	In afternoon, two sections of 253rd M.G. Coy relieved No 3 & 4 Sections, who returned to billets at FOUQUEREUIL EVERMELLES	S.L.C.
FOUQUEREUIL	15/8/16	-	No 1 & 2 Sections moved to billets at FOUQUEREUIL. Coy. H.Q and No 3 & 4 Sections were relieved by 253rd M.G. Coy in morning, and moved to FOUQUEREUIL. Transport joined up at SAILLY LABOURSE & moved to lines at FOUQUEREUIL. Weather very wet. Billets fairly good.	P.L.C
	16/8/16	-	Sections paraded in morning for cleaning guns, kits, etc.	P.L.C.
	17/8/16	-	Sections paraded for arms and gun drill	P.L.C
	18/8/16	-	Company paraded for baths at SAILLY LABOURSE & O.R. join the Coy. from GRANTHAM.	S.L.C.
	19/8/16	-	Construction of horse-standings in transport field is begun. One section is detailed each day, in billets, for this work.	P.L.C
	20/8/16	-	Church parades in morning. In afternoon, three men of the Coy. who were not able to battle on 18th inst., paraded in bath at FOUQUIERES.	P.L.C.
	21/8/16	-	2/Lieut. A.D. Cumming + 1 O.R. join the Coy. from GRANTHAM. Medical inspection of Coy. in morning. O.C. Coy. and Os.C. No 2, 3, & 4 Sections visit trenches of HOHENZOLLERN Sector. Coy. Dry Canteen started.	
	22/8/16	-	Paid Parades as usual.	S.L.C. S.L.C.
VERMELLES	23/8/16	-	No 2, 3, & 4 Sections moved off to trenches at 4.0 A.M., to relieve 10 guns of 27th M.G Coy in HOHENZOLLERN Sector. Lt. Fletcher & Higham with 3 guns took over positions in reserve line on right, Lt. Poulter + Beachman with 4 guns took over positions in reserve line on left, Lts. Perkins and Cumming with 3 guns took over positions in Village line. Lt. Perkins also had command of 2 guns left by 23rd Coy in Village line.	

Army Form C. 2118.

WAR DIARY
or
INTELLIGENCE SUMMARY

(Erase heading not required.)

Instructions regarding War Diaries and Intelligence Summaries are contained in F. S. Regs., Part II and the Staff Manual respectively. Title Pages will be prepared in manuscript.

Place	Date	Hour	Summary of Events and Information	Remarks and references to Appendices
VERMELLES	23/8/16 (contd)	-	Coy. H.Q. with No.1 Section Transport moved out at 7.30 A.M. West Transport lines at LABOURSE. Coy. H.Q. in cellars of Brewery at VERMELLES. In afternoon 4 guns Donnan & Sulley with 3 guns of No.3 Section relieved 3 guns of 97 M.G.Coy in HULLUCH Sector, being lent to 97th Bde. for 3 days.	S.L.C.
	24/8/16	-	15 and of No.1 Section + 4 guns of 23rd Coy were in Reserve at Brewery.	S.L.C.
	25/8/16	-	On this and following nights the 3 sections carried out indirect fire on cross-roads, tramways, tracks, & other "tender spots". At 8.30 P.M. Coy H.Q. received "S.O.S. G.12.5 – G.12.7." "S.O.S Cancelled" received at 10.45 P.M. During the night 2 raids were carried out on the Bde. front, after bombardments, there were some artillery retaliation by the enemy, in the course of which 3 O.R. were killed and 1 O.R. wounded, belonging to No.2 Section.	S.L.C.
	26/8/16	-	In afternoon, the 5 guns lent to 97th Bde. returned to the Coy's. The 2 guns of No 3 Section proceeded to the Village Line, relieving the 2 guns left by the 23rd Coy; the 3 guns of No.1 Section remained at the Brewery, relieving the guns of the 23rd Coy left there in Reserve.	S.L.C.
	27/8/16 28/8/16	-	Everything normal. Lt. Beechman with 2 O.R. left to attend "Anti-Gas" Course. No.1 Section relieved No.2 Section in right of reserve line. No.2 Section relieved No.4 Section in left of Reserve Line. No.4 Section relieved No.3 Section in Village Line. No.3 Section went into Reserve at Brewery.	S.L.C. F.L.C.
	29/8/16	-	In afternoon Thunderstorms, with very heavy rain. One emplacement in reserve line partially fell in; but trenches drained well. Some cellars at Brewery both were washed out.	S.L.C.
	30/8/16	-	Very windy, cold, & wet. 3 O.R. joined the Coy. from GRANTHAM.	S.L.C. F.L.C.
	31/8/16	-	No.3 Section relieved No.1 Section in right of reserve line. No.1 Section relieved No.2 Section in left of reserve line. No.2 Section relieved No.4 Section in Village Line. No.4 Section went into Reserve at Brewery. Weather fine.	S.L.C.

8th, Division.

24th, Brigade.

24th, Machine Gun Co.

September, 1916.

24 M G Coy
Vol x 9

WAR DIARY by Captain F.E.C.Lewis
for the Month of September 1916.

Army Form C. 2118.

WAR DIARY
or
INTELLIGENCE SUMMARY
(Erase heading not required.)

Instructions regarding War Diaries and Intelligence Summaries are contained in F. S. Regs., Part II. and the Staff Manual respectively. Title Pages will be prepared in manuscript.

Place	Date	Hour	Summary of Events and Information	Remarks and references to Appendices
VERMELLES	Sept 1st	—	In the morning H.Q. Nos 3 and 4 Sections and 3 men from each section in the trenches went to MOYECRES for Baths. Lt. Beechman and 2. O.R. report for Anti Gas School. Situation normal. Lt. Higham takes over duties of T.O.	T.O.f. M.I.
"	2nd		No 4 Section relieved No 3 Section in the right of the Reserve line. No 3. relieved No 1 Section in the left of the Reserve line. No 1 Section relieved No 2 Section in the Village line.	I.O.f.
	3rd			
	4th		No 2. Section came back to BREWRY. Situation normal. 2nd Lt Bailes went for course B.M.G. School at CAMIERS. Situation normal.	I.O.f.
	5th			I.O.f.
	6th		No 2 Section relieved No 4 Section in the right of the Reserve line. No 4 relieved No 3 in the left of Reserve line. No 3 Relieved No 1 in the Village line. No 1 Section came to the BREWRY.	I.O.f.

Army Form C. 2118.

WAR DIARY
or
INTELLIGENCE SUMMARY
(Erase heading not required.)

Instructions regarding War Diaries and Intelligence Summaries are contained in F. S. Regs., Part II. and the Staff Manual respectively. Title Pages will be prepared in manuscript.

Place	Date	Hour	Summary of Events and Information	Remarks and references to Appendices
VERMELLES	7th 8th	—	Ordinary Parades and cleaning up cellars etc.	TCR.
FOUQUER EUIL	8th	-	The Company is relieved by the 25th M.G.Coy. Relief complete by 12.15 pm. The Company moves back billets in FOUQUER-EUIL arriving there 5.15 pm.	TCR.
"	9th		Inspection parades. Work carried on on the Transport lines where no work had been done by the other 2 companies for 16t days.	TCR.
"	10th		Working Parties 75 men all day at HESDIGNEUL Aerodrome. Work done on horse lines.	TCR.
"	11th		Working party same as 10th. 12 Serjeants M.C.C. been sent to BASE.	TCR.
"	12th		75 men working party MINX as before. 25 men MINX YARD.	TCR.
"	13th		Same as 12th.	TCR.
"	14th		16 men on working parties. O.C. Coy. 2nd Lt Cainwood and 2nd Beech-attend lecture at Arty School. GOSNAY.	TCR.

WAR DIARY
or
INTELLIGENCE SUMMARY

(Erase heading not required.)

Army Form C. 2118.

Place	Date	Hour	Summary of Events and Information	Remarks and references to Appendices
FOUQUEREUIL	Sept. 15th	—	Cleaning up Parades. O.C. Coy and Lt Hitcher visit the Trenches	nil
"	16th	—	The Company marched as far as SAILLY LABOURSE on the way to relieve 23rd M.G. Coy. Relief cancelled. The Company returns to billets in FOUQUEREUIL.	nil
VERMELLES	17th	—	The Company relieves the 23rd M.G. Coy in the line. Sector Relief complete 12.15 pm. 10 guns in the line. Lt Gontaud goes to 1st Army School of Instruction. O.C. Coy visits Trenches. Ordinary Usual Parades for sections.	nil nil
"	18th	—	in MG – VERMELLES.	nil
"	19th	—	Situation Normal.	nil
"	20th	—	Baths for 50 men at VERMELLES BREWRY.	nil
"	21st	—	Nos 3 and 4 Sections relieve Nos. 1 and 2 respectively.	nil
"	22nd	—	Situation Normal. Usual indirect fire carried out. Lt Britz returns from M.G. School at CAMIERS.	nil
"	23rd	—	Situation normal. Usual parades for sections in VERMELLES.	nil

WAR DIARY
or
INTELLIGENCE SUMMARY

Army Form C. 2118.

Place	Date	Hour	Summary of Events and Information	Remarks and references to Appendices
VERMELLES	Sept. 24th	—	Situation normal. Totals arrived drafts instructed in mechanism. Remainder carried on with usual fatigues.	T.Ch.
	25th	—	Situation normal. Relief takes place. No 1 relieves No 4. No 2 relieves No 3 section. Relief complete by 4.15 p.m.	T.Ch.
	26th	—	Situation normal. Lt. Donan goes on leave to England. 2 Guns go to HIGHLAND TRENCH.	T.Ch.
		11 a.m.	Our 6's increasing and 8.2 Trench Mortars.	T.Ch.
		2 p.m.	Hostile enemy activity, 15 Crumps and Trench Mortars.	
	27th	—	Enemy rather more active. Artillery and Hostile Artillery. Shields Patrols of 1 N.C.O	T.Ch.
	28th	—	Men Patrols as usual. Hostile Artillery Shields. Patrols of 1 N.C.O and men each to dam 3 Communication Trenches Steilzug, 2 Guns return from HIGHLAND TRENCH.	T.Ch.
	29th	—	Relief takes place. No. 3 relieves No 1. No. 2 relieve No. 2 Section. Relief Complete 4.15 p.m.	T.Ch.
	30th	—	Situation normal. Parties again work Communication Trenches to clear of I.N.C.O and 2 men at 6 p.m. to take old slats of trench boards in CHAPEL ALLEY trenches.	T.Ch.

8th, Division.

24th, Brigade

24th, Machine Gun Co.

October, 1916.

Vol 10
8th Bn

War Diary
of the
24th M.G. Company
for the Month
of October 1916

WAR DIARY

24th Machine Gun Coy

October 1916

Place	Date	Hour	Summary of Events and Information	Remarks and references to Appendices
VERMELLES	Oct 1st 1916		Very quiet. Hardly any enemy activity of any kind. Usual parades. Lt. Rowles and 2/Lt. proceeded to Divl. Anti Gas School at GOSNAY. Indirect fire carried out as usual.	AM
"	2nd		"W" Day. Artillery bombardment. Divisional scheme. Section parades – Indirect fire. Party on trench maintenance – communication trenches in Brigade sector.	
"	3rd		No. 1 section relieved No. 4 section and No. 2 section relieved No. 3 section. Baths at VERMELLES BREWERY. 24th Field Ambulance Advanced Dressing Station.	
"			"X" Day. Artillery bombardment. Shell from enemy trench mortar fell near HOHENZOLLERN REDOUBT. It burst without any audible detonation and sent out clouds of smoke which drifted back towards the enemy lines. Indirect fire during the night was continued.	
"	4th		"Y" Day. Usual section parades. Training of new drafts. Artillery bombardment. Indirect fire in conjunction with Divisional scheme on roads and communication trenches behind the enemy lines.	PR
"	5th		"Z" Day. Gas was discharged three times and twice more during the evening. Artillery bombardment increased to intense and machine guns cooperated. Indirect fire was carried out as usual at intervals during the night on dumps and tracks spots behind the enemy lined. Usual section parades. Nos 3 & 4 sections and transport were fixed out.	JOb

WAR DIARY
INTELLIGENCE SUMMARY

Army Form C. 2118.

Place	Date	Hour	Summary of Events and Information	Remarks and references to Appendices
VERMELLES	Oct 6th		Usual Section parades. Lieut. J.R. Bowler + 2 O.R. returned from Anti-Gas School. Raid by 23rd Brigade. Lecture on aeroplane photographs at SAILLY LABOURSE by Corps Intelligence Officer attended by 4 Officers and 4 O.R. Capt. F.E.C. Lewis proceeded on leave of absence to United Kingdom. Indirect fire was carried out at intervals during the night on roads and communication trenches behind the enemy lines.	NCL
"	7th		Baths at NOYELLES allotted to Company. No. 3 Section relieved No. 1 Section in VILLAGE LINE. No. 4 Section relieved No. 2 Section. Indirect fire was carried out at intervals during the night on various tender spots behind the enemy lines.	NCL
"	8th		Usual Section parades. Nos. 1 + 2 Sections were paid out. Indirect fire was carried out during the night on dumps, tramways and roads behind the enemy lines.	NCL

Army Form C. 2118.

WAR DIARY
or
INTELLIGENCE SUMMARY.
(Erase heading not required.)

Place	Date	Hour	Summary of Events and Information	Remarks and references to Appendices
VERMELLES	9/X/16		Nos 3 & 4 Sections in trenches. QUARRIES Sector. Nos 1 & 2 Sections resting in billets. Lieut R.H. Neal Introduced Regt posted to Company as 2nd in command. 1 O.R. from 35 Coy via Divl. S. & Contailed. 1 O.R. to 8th M.G. Coy.	TRC
	10"		Trenches visited by officers of the 12nd M.G. Coy. 21st Division. Company relieved by 62nd Coy. moved to billets in FOUQUEREUIL.	ROC
FOUQUEREUIL	11"		Company resting in billets. Baths at FOUQUIERES allotted to Company. Gun equipment cleaned. Usual section parades.	
	12"		Resting in billets. All attached men except 5 per battalion were sent back to their regiments.	8 Div. G. 34.
	13"		Lieut W. Orkney Stewart transferred attd 2nd M.G. Coy, proceeded to M.G. Training Centre GRANTHAM. Limbers packed ready for move.	
	14"		Entrained at FOUQUEREUIL station. Detrained at KONGPRÉ near ABBEVILLE. Marched to billets at HOCQUINCOURT via SOREL & HALLENCOURT.	ARC
HOCQUINCOURT	15"		Company resting at HOCQUINCOURT Sector parade, guns, gun equipment and limbers cleaned.	
	16"		Company marched to SOREL and moved by 'bus to VILLE near ALBERT. Marched to camp in SAND PITS nr MEAULTE. Transport moving separately marched from HOCQUINCOURT to AILLY-SUR-SOMME.	
MEAULTE	17"		Tactical training in FRICOURT area. O.C. Company visited trenches near GUEDECOURT. Transport marched from AILLY-SUR-SOMME to SANDPITS and rejoined Company.	

Army Form C. 2118.

WAR DIARY
or
INTELLIGENCE SUMMARY
(Erase heading not required.)

Instructions regarding War Diaries and Intelligence Summaries are contained in F. S. Regs., Part II. and the Staff Manual respectively. Title Pages will be prepared in manuscript.

Place	Date	Hour	Summary of Events and Information	Remarks and references to Appendices
MÉAULTE	18th Oct 1916		Company resting under canvas. Commanding Officers' conference. Guns & gun apparent cleaned.	
"	19th		Maps & transport of 71st M.G. Coy at MONTAUBAN visited by officers of the Company. Company travelled to MONTAUBAN where bivouacked before section relieved 71st M.G. Company, & bivouaced in trenches to right of GUEDECOURT. Advanced company Hqrs near DELVILLE WOOD. Transport lines at MONTAUBAN. Nos 1, 2, & 3 sections in trenches. No. 4 section in reserve at Advanced Coy H.Q. 2nd Lt Boulter & Lummis at A.C.M.Q. & Lt Beechnam at MONTAUBAN.	
DELVILLE WOOD	20th		Relief complete about 6 P.M. Company headquarters moved to BERNAFAY-FLERS road. Capt Levis returned from leave. 2nd Lt F.J.R. Boulter admitted to Hospital. Casualties Wounded 1 O.R. Missing 1 O.R.	
"	21st		No. 4 Section relieved No. 1 Section in trenches. Rest Company relieved 2 Lt Donner in trenches	
"	22nd		2 Lt Beechnam relieved 2 Lt Hebden in trenches. Several new dugouts were built.	
"	23rd		2/Lt F.P. Ellis, Durham Light Infantry attd M.G.C. joined company. 1st Durham Light Infantry attacked in front of GUEDECOURT. 2 Lieut Fletcher had 2 guns in readiness to take over and 2nd Lt Beechnam had 2 guns in readiness to take over & 2nd Lieut Beechnam took one gun over but had to come back owing to the front elected not being properly consolidated	

Army Form C. 2118.

WAR DIARY
or
INTELLIGENCE SUMMARY

(Erase heading not required.)

Instructions regarding War Diaries and Intelligence Summaries are contained in F. S. Regs., Part II. and the Staff Manual respectively. Title Pages will be prepared in manuscript.

Place	Date	Hour	Summary of Events and Information	Remarks and references to Appendices
DELVILLE WOOD	23rd (contd)		Several good targets were offered and fired on. 2 guns were buried by our own artillery fire. Owing largely to the gallantry of S.M. Rice 2nd But Rifles and Lce Cpl Tomlinson 24 M.G. Coy all the men were dugout alive. Casualties Killed 1 O.R. Wounded 7 O.R. (including 3 at duty) 1 O.R. reported missing 20th not reported	ASR
	24th		2 guns + gun pit dugout in RAINBOW TRENCH near Batt. H.A. 2nd But Rants. 2/Lieut Fletcher proceeded to M.G. Training Centre GRANTHAM. 2 teams of no 3 Section came out to Reserve. Casualties Wounded 2 O.R.	
	25th		® 2 teams no 2 Section + remaining 2 teams no 3 Section came out to reserve. 2/Lt Donovan returned 2/Lt Polly in trenches. Casualties: 2 Lt Ellis + 3 O.R. admitted to hospital.	
	26th		Ten guns in trenches. Remaining teams resting in dugouts near DELVILLE WOOD. Casualties. Sick 5 O.R.	

Army Form C. 2118.

WAR DIARY
or
INTELLIGENCE SUMMARY
(Erase heading not required.)

Instructions regarding War Diaries and Intelligence Summaries are contained in F. S. Regs., Part II. and the Staff Manual respectively. Title Pages will be prepared in manuscript.

Place	Date	Hour	Summary of Events and Information	Remarks and references to Appendices
DELVILLE WOOD	27th Oct		Two teams of No. 3 Section relieved two teams of No. 2 Section on night of CLOUDY TRENCH. 2 Lt. fully relieved 2 Lt. Bunning. CASUALTIES: Sick 1 O.R.	
	28th		Ten guns were in the line and six teams resting at Company Hdqrs. in valley between DELVILLE WOOD and FLERS. Three prisoners came in to right hand gun. All quiet. Casualties Sick 1 O.R.	
	29th		Two teams of No. 3 Section + two teams of No. 2 Section relieved No. 4 Section in SMINE TRENCH (left battalion). The two right hand guns were then withdrawn to a position near the left battalion hdqrs. A Russian prisoner came in to right hand gun during the night. Indirect fire was carried out on LE TRANSLOY - BAPAUME Rd. at N.18.d.2.7½ (all maps). Casualties Wounded 1 O.R. Sick 2 O.R.	
"	30th		Ten guns in the line. Six in front line system and four in redoubt near each battalion headquarters. Five guns in reserve near Bde. hdqrs.	

Army Form C. 2118.

WAR DIARY
or
INTELLIGENCE SUMMARY

(Erase heading not required.)

Place	Date	Hour	Summary of Events and Information	Remarks and references to Appendices
DELVILLE WOOD	30TH (cont)		A Bavarian officer and his servant came in to the night. He gave no information of any value. Front line system was heavily shelled during the morning. A barrage was put on the valley behind the trenches as usual during the morning and evening "stand to". O.C. 52nd Company of relieving division came up to see trenches.	1Ch.
"	31ST		52nd Company arrived to relieve company. Trenches shelled again and barrage put on valley just behind our trenches. Own heavy guns were again active. Guns fired on enemy trenches during the night. No. 4 section went back to "C" camp when 52nd Franks gun company relieved Company. Company released by 52nd Franks gun company. Company moved back to its bivouacs at "C" camp during the night. Casualties. Wounded 4 O.R.	1Ch.

24.11.16 J.P. Kerr Capt.
O.C. 24 M.G. Coy

8th, Division.

24th, Brigade.

24th, Machine Gun Co.

November, 1916.

To:-

D. A. G. Base

Herewith - War Diary of the 24th Machine

Gun Company for the Month of November 1916.

J.B.C. Lewis. Captain

3-12-16.

Comdg-24th M. G. Company.

WAR DIARY

of the

24th Machine Gun Company.

by

Captain. F. E. C. Lewis

for the month of November 1916

Army Form C. 2118.

WAR DIARY
or
INTELLIGENCE SUMMARY
(Erase heading not required.)

Place	Date	Hour	Summary of Events and Information	Remarks and references to Appendices
TRONES WOOD	Nov 1st		Company moved by sections back to SANDPITS CAMP near MEAULTE.	
MEAULTE	2nd		Draft of 15 O.R. arrived. Camp improved and cleared up. Latrines and cookhouses built.	
	3rd		Guns and gun pits cleaned in morning. Military medals presented by G.O.C. 8 Div. 2 Lt. Campbell 3rd Somerset Light Infantry and 2 Lt. R.L. Walbyton 3/4th Batt. Lincolnshire Regt. (T.F.) attd. M.G. Corps joined for duty.	
	4th		Company resting in camp. Camp cleaned up. Inspection by G.O.C. 24th Infantry Brigade.	
	5th		2 Lt. Beecham + 2 O.R. to CAMIERS on machine gun course. Paraded at 10 A.M. and marched to huts near CARNOY via MAMETZ & MONTAUBAN, in a camp with 1st Worcesters and 1st Sherwood Foresters. Transport in CARNOY.	
CARNOY	6th		Relieved 100th Company in trenches to right of LESBOEUFS. Left camp at 2 P.M. and moved up to trenches.	

WAR DIARY or INTELLIGENCE SUMMARY

Army Form C. 2118.

Place	Date	Hour	Summary of Events and Information	Remarks and references to Appendices
	Nov 6th (contd)		Two guns of No 4 section in front line. Two guns of No 4 section and two guns of No 2 section under 2/Lt Wallington & Sully in support in ANTELOPE TRENCH. No 3 section in reserve in OX TRENCH under 2/Lt Cumming. 1 N.C.O. + 3 men per gun team being left at transport lines at BRICQUETERIE near BERNAFAY WOOD. Coy H.Q. in GUILLEMONT. 1 days iron ration, extra spare man in L.G. teams. No 1 section and ½ No 2 section was taken in by teams. No 1 section remained at transport under 2/Lt Dorman. 2/Lt Cornwell was liaison officer between pack transport and Coy H.Q. O.C. Company visited trenches with brigade major during the evening. Hostile shelling decreased. Our artillery were very active as usual.	
LESBOEUFS	7th			
	8th		The following reliefs took place in the afternoon and evening:— No 3 section relieved No 4 section in front line and in right of ANTELOPE TRENCH. Half of No 2 section relieved the other half of No 2 section in ANTELOPE TRENCH. No 4 section returned to OX TRENCH on relief & ½ No 2 section under 2 Lt Sully to transport under 2 Lt Dorman	

Army Form C. 2118.

WAR DIARY
or
INTELLIGENCE SUMMARY

(Erase heading not required.)

Instructions regarding War Diaries and Intelligence Summaries are contained in F. S. Regs., Part II. and the Staff Manual respectively. Title Pages will be prepared in manuscript.

Place	Date	Hour	Summary of Events and Information	Remarks and references to Appendices
LESBOEUFS	7th 8	5.45 P.M.	Considerable artillery activity to right of GUEDECOURT	
	6th 6th	6.15 P.M.	ANTELOPE TRENCH heavily shelled.	
		6.30	Considerable artillery activity in front of LESBOEUFS. CASUALTIES — 1 O.R.	
	9th	2-4 P.M.	GINCHY CORNER shelled. Company relieved by 25th M.G. Coy. O.C. 25th Coy came up in morning to arrange relief.	
		7 P.M.	Relief complete. On relief sections handed to tents in huts near CARNOY (SOUTH CAMP)	
CARNOY	10th		Company resting in camp. Foot inspection. Cleaning up guns and rifles cleared.	
	11th		Company ready in camp. Section parades, rifle inspection, gun drill and light tripods. Signallers practised with buzzer. G.O.C. Brigade came round with Brigade Major during morning parade. C.O.'s conference at bde. H.Q.	

WAR DIARY or INTELLIGENCE SUMMARY

Army Form C. 2118.

Place	Date	Hour	Summary of Events and Information	Remarks and references to Appendices
CARNOY	12th Aug		O.C. Company visited HdQrs 23RD H.Q. Coy. in GUILLEMONT to arrange relief. Church parade, communion and voluntary service in morning. Gun limbers were sent up to transport lines. 5 O.R. (drivers) joined and 3 O.R. for 2nd East Lancashire Regt.	
	13th		Company moved by sections from camp near CARNOY to GUILLEMONT STATION (Bde H.Q.) where guides from 23RD H.Q. Coy. were provided to take company 3 sections up to trenches. No 3 section under 2Lt Cumming were left at GUILLEMONT STATION in reserve dug-outs. Two days rations were taken into trenches. No 1 section under 2Lt Doran was in front with 2 guns in front line and 2 guns in support line. No 2 section under 2Lt Tully was in support in WINDMILL TRENCH. No 4 section under 2Lt Walker was in reserve at Company HdQrs in SERPENTINE TRENCH (FLERS LINE) 2Lt Campbell acted as liaison officer between Bde H.Q. and pack mules transport. No 1 section heavily shelled while going up. (Casualties killed 2 S.R. Wounded 2 O.R. (1 at duty))	

WAR DIARY
INTELLIGENCE SUMMARY

Army Form C. 2118.

Place	Date	Hour	Summary of Events and Information	Remarks and references to Appendices
LESBOEUFS	14th		Hostile shelling against LESBOEUFS. Our support trenches were intermittently shelled during the day. Enemy aeroplane was brought down between LESBOEUFS and MORVAL. Our artillery shelled LE TRANSLOY-BEAULENCOURT Road continuously during the day.	
	15th		The following reliefs were carried out during the afternoon. No 4 section relieved No 1 section. No 3 section relieved No 2 section. On relief No 1 section took up positions in SERPENTINE TRENCH and No 2 sections returned to reserve dugouts near tote H.A. at GUILLEMONT Station. Relief was again stalled. Adjutant of the 88th Bn. 9 Coy 29th Division came up to arrange relief. Casualties. Wounded 2 O.R.	
	16th		Officers of the 88th Company came up to trenches. No gun position in WINDMILL TRENCH taken over by 1st Guards Brigade M.G Coy. 4 guns moved to JOHN BULL trench, 4 teams of 88th Company came to 4 trenches and our 4 teams came back to Coy H.D. in SERPENTINE TRENCH on relief.	

WAR DIARY
or
INTELLIGENCE SUMMARY

Army Form C. 2118.

Place	Date	Hour	Summary of Events and Information	Remarks and references to Appendices
LESBOEUFS	17th Nov		Remainder of teams excepting one man per gun were sent out of trenches. 2nd Lieut Dornan hauled party back to NORTH CAMP near CARNOY.	
CARNOY	18th		Company relieved by 88th M.G. Coy. Section marched to NORTH CAMP. Cooks cart, mess cart, 13th limber and 7 riding horses were sent on under 2nd Lt Bagnell to march by road to XV Corps are Company marched to billets in MEAULTE. 2nd Lt Cumming went on in advance to arrange billets. Spare kit was fetched for dump.	
MEAULTE	19th		Section parades, cleaning guns, sorting kit etc. Rifle inspection. Baths for fifty men. Transport lines moved closer to billets.	
	20th		Move to manoeuvre area XV Corps. 2nd Lt Cumming went on in advance by first train to arrange billets. Spare kit taken to EDGE HILL station DERNANCOURT on a motor lorry. Company marched to EDGE HILL station where Limbers were carted. Stores and labours loaded on to 3rd train. 2nd Lt Wallington went by this train to act as unloading party at PONT REMY	

WAR DIARY
or
INTELLIGENCE SUMMARY

Army Form C. 2118.

(Erase heading not required.)

Place	Date	Hour	Summary of Events and Information	Remarks and references to Appendices
	20th (contd.)		4 limbers had to go by road under Lt. Hyslop as there was not room on the train.	
	21st		Remainder of company entrained on 2nd train (personnel) at 6.0 p.m. with 2nd Bn. Lancashire Regt. & 2nd Northamptonshire Regt. Train went through AMIENS to OISEMONT where spare kit was dumped. Company started from OISEMONT to billets at FRESNEVILLE.	
		10 A.M. (0.30)	Very good billets — all horses under cover. 2/Lt Banfield's party rejoiced. 2/Lt Wilkinson's party rejoined.	
FRESNEVILLE	22nd		Company resting in billets. Cleaning up, cleaning guns, rifles, limbers etc. Lieut Hyslop arrived with 4 limbers which had marched by road. Spare kit arrived.	
	23rd		Cleaned rifles, guns, gun kit, limbers etc. Rifle drill and more practice for 4 fellows. Riding school for all officers. 1 O.R. to HAVRE to transport course.	
	24th		Lieut Heale + 3 O.R. on leave to England.	

Army Form C. 2118.

WAR DIARY
or
INTELLIGENCE SUMMARY

(Erase heading not required.)

Instructions regarding War Diaries and Intelligence Summaries are contained in F. S. Regs., Part II. and the Staff Manual respectively. Title Pages will be prepared in manuscript.

Place	Date	Hour	Summary of Events and Information	Remarks and references to Appendices
FRESNEVILLE	Nov 25th		Remaining gun kit cleaned. Limbers cleaned & oiled.	
	26th		Physical training 7.30 a.m. Stoppages & mechanism in morning. Lecture on use of rangefinder by Lt. Cumming in afternoon.	
	27th		Running drill 7.30 a.m. Arms & gun drill in morning. Football in afternoon. Lt Cumming to G.H.Q. for M.G. course.	
	28th		Physical training 7.30 a.m. Revolver practise & gas helmet drill in morning.	
	29th		Running drill 7.30 a.m. Squad & gun drill in morning.	
	30th		Physical training 7.30 a.m. Belt filling & elementary tests (aimed) during morning	

WAR DIARY
or
INTELLIGENCE SUMMARY

Army Form C. 2118.

Place	Date	Hour	Summary of Events and Information	Remarks and references to Appendices
TRONES WOOD	1st		Company moved by sections back to SANDPITS CAMP near MÉAULTE. Draft of 15 O.R. arrived.	
MÉAULTE	2nd		Camp improved and cleared up. Latrines and cookhouses built.	
	3rd		Guns and gun pits cleaned in morning. Military medals presented by G.O.C. 8th Divn. 2 Lt Campbell 3rd Somerset Light Infantry and 2 Lt A.L. Walkington 3/4 7th Batt. Lincolnshire Regt. (T.F.) attd M.G. Corps joined for duty.	
	4th		Company resting in camp. Camp cleaned up. Inspection by G.O.C. 24th Infantry Brigade.	
	5th		2 Lt Beacham + 2 O.R. to CAMIERS on machine gun course. Paraded at 10 A.M. and marched to huts near CARNOY near MAMETZ & MONTAUBAN, in a camp with 1st Worcesters and 1st Sherwood Foresters. Transport in CARNOY.	
CARNOY	6th		Relieved 100th Company in trenches to right of LESBOEUFS. Left camp at 2 P.M. and moved up to trenches.	J.C. Lewis Cpt. M.G. Coy O.C. 249. M.G. Coy 3.D.16.

8th, Division.

24th, Brigade.

24th, Machine Gun Co.

December, 1916.

D.A.G. Base.

Herewith- War Diary of the
24TH M.G. Company.

R.J. Wheeler Lieut for Captain
Comdg 24TH M.G. Co

2/4/17.

War Diary of the
24th Machine Gun Company.
for the Month of
December, 1916
by
Captain F. C. C. Lewis

Army Form C. 2118.

WAR DIARY
or
INTELLIGENCE SUMMARY
(Erase heading not required.)

Place	Date	Hour	Summary of Events and Information	Remarks and references to Appendices
Fresneville	1916 Dec 1st		Running drill 7.30 a.m. Mechanism & revolver practice during morning.	
	2nd		Physical training 7.30 a.m. Drill with limbers in training area. Brigade cross country run.	
	3rd		Church parades.	
	4th		Physical training 7.30 a.m. Judging distance, visual training & range finding in morning.	
	5th		Running drill 7.30 a.m. Practise on range in morning. Belt filling in afternoon.	
	6th		Physical training 7.30 a.m. Mechanism & stripping (timed) during morning. Football in running in afternoon.	
	7th		Running drill 7.30 a.m. Practise on range in morning	

Army Form C. 2118.

WAR DIARY
or
INTELLIGENCE SUMMARY
(Erase heading not required.)

Instructions regarding War Diaries and Intelligence Summaries are contained in F. S. Regs., Part II. and the Staff Manual respectively. Title Pages will be prepared in manuscript.

Place	Date	Hour	Summary of Events and Information	Remarks and references to Appendices
Fresneville	Dec 8th		Physical Training 7.30 am. Practise on range during morning. Belt filling in afternoon	
	9th		Running drill 7.30 am. Company marched to Selincourt to see finish of Brigade cross country run. Lt. Beechman & 2 O.R. to England on leave.	Lt Heale + 3 O.R. returned from leave.
	10th		Church parades.	
	11th		Running drill 7.30 am. Practise on range. Instruction for range finders in morning. Belt filling during afternoon.	
	12th		Physical Training 7.30 am. Morning Parade cancelled 12 noon for inspection by G.O.C. 8th Divn.	Cleaning up during afternoon
	13th		Running Drill 7.30 am. During day Company took up positions of defense around village	

Army Form C. 2118.

WAR DIARY
or
INTELLIGENCE SUMMARY
(Erase heading not required.)

Instructions regarding War Diaries and Intelligence Summaries are contained in F. S. Regs., Part II. and the Staff Manual respectively. Title Pages will be prepared in manuscript.

Place	Date	Hour	Summary of Events and Information	Remarks and references to Appendices
FRESNEVILLE	Dec 14th	7.0 A.M.	Company resting in Hornoy area XV Corps in billets at FRESNEVILLE. Detachment at SOMME. Physical training. Squad and rifle drill or training area "R". Gun drill with numbers. Running practice and football in afternoon.	
	15th	7.30 A.M.	Running drill. Mechanism and stoppages. Lecture to officers and N.C.O.'s on "Morale" by Brigadier General Edwards also instructed officers on Mining School. Football match with 1st Bn. The Sherwood Foresters at SELINCOURT. 2 O.R. on leave to England.	
	16th	7.10 A.M.	Physical drill. Nos 2,3, & 4 sections on range, grouping practice (5 rnds) and swinging traverse were carried out. No 1 Section and Mgrs. balled and 2 to Bruning and 2.O.R. washed clothes. Lieut Stephen went on leave. Returned from Hotchkiss gun course.	
	17th	7.30 A.M.	Church parade (C. of E.) in loft at Hdqrs. R.C.'s and nonconformists went to services with 2nd Bn Northamptonshire Regt at VILLERS.	
	18th	7.30 A.M.	Physical drill. Nos 1,3, and 4 sections on range. Grouping practice (10 rnds) and swinging traverse were carried out. No 2 section bathing and washing clothes. Ball shilling in afternoon.	

Army Form C. 2118.

WAR DIARY
or
INTELLIGENCE SUMMARY
(Erase heading not required.)

Instructions regarding War Diaries and Intelligence Summaries are contained in F. S. Regs., Part II. and the Staff Manual respectively. Title Pages will be prepared in manuscript.

Place	Date	Hour	Summary of Events and Information	Remarks and references to Appendices
FRESNEVILLE	19th		Running drill. Section parades, range practice, gun drill, and mechanism. No 3 section bathing and washing clothes. Running practice and football.	
	20th		I.O.R. returned from Transport course. Draft of 5 O.R. joined.	
	21st		Physical drill. Open order drill with sections and park animals. Football in afternoon. Sgt Higginbottom to take over duties of C.Q.M.S.	
	22nd		Running drill. Squad and rifle drill or having tea. "R" Coy takes over with Lieut Bennett. Mechanism. Football in afternoon.	
	23rd		Physical drill, mechanism and stoppages during morning. Football match against 25th Machine Gun Company.	
	24th		Running drill. Range practice. Swinging traverse. Roll filling in afternoon. C.Q.M.S. Humphries left on promotion.	
	25th		Church parade. Commanding Officers' conference at Bde H.Q. at 11 A.M. Inter geared football match v 25th Machine Gun Company.	
			Classification by Inspection parades.	

Army Form C. 2118.

WAR DIARY
or
INTELLIGENCE SUMMARY

(Erase heading not required.)

Instructions regarding War Diaries and Intelligence Summaries are contained in F. S. Regs., Part II. and the Staff Manual respectively. Title Pages will be prepared in manuscript.

Place	Date	Hour	Summary of Events and Information	Remarks and references to Appendices
FRESNEVILLE	26th Dec		Range, swinging traverse. Inspection of rifles, gas helmets, box respirators, field dressings and emergency rations. Guns stripped out belts filled in afternoon.	
	27th		Physical drill. Range practice for men armed with rifles. Grand drill for men armed with revolvers. Transport paraded at 8.45 A.M. and marched to starting point at CAMPS-EN-AMIENS. marched through MOLLIENS VIDAME to OISSY where horses were watered and fed, marched through CAVILLON, FOURDRINOY, BREILLY and AILLY-SUR-SOMME to billets in ~~VAUX-SUR-SOMME~~ ST SAUVEUR.	
	28th		Inspection of brigade at SELINCOURT by G.O.C. VIII Division. transport marched from ST SAUVEUR through ARGOEUVRES and AMIENS to DAOURS where horses were watered and fed. marched through CORBIE to billets in VAUX-SUR-SOMME.	
	29th		Company entrained at DISEMONT. Detrained at EDGEHILL STATION near DERNANCOURT and marched to CAMP III near BRAY. transport marched from VAUX to CAMP III near BRAY where company was rejoined. Two large huts capable of holding 150 men each were allotted to the company.	
	30th		Inspection of gas helmets, box respirators, field dressings, rifles and iron rations. Company marched to CAMP 16 near MARICOURT. Lt. Beckham / 2 O.R. returned from leave.	

Army Form C. 2118.

WAR DIARY
or
INTELLIGENCE SUMMARY
(Erase heading not required.)

Place	Date	Hour	Summary of Events and Information	Remarks and references to Appendices
CAMP	31st Dec		Units and camp cleaned up. Guns and gun pits cleaned. Transport lines improved. Hunters wished commanding officer and the officers a Happy Christmas and a Very Happy New Year.	

Vol 13.

War Diary
of the
24th M.G Coy.
for the month
of January 1917
by
Major F E C Lewis.

WAR DIARY or INTELLIGENCE SUMMARY

Army Form C. 2118.

Place	Date	Hour	Summary of Events and Information	Remarks and references to Appendices
CAMP 16 BRONFAY FARM	Jan 1st		Section Parades. Officers Company visited by XII Corps Machine Gun Officer. Commanding Officers conferences evening. I.O.R. returned from leave.	no appx
	2nd		Company resting in huts in Bronfay Reserve in Camp 16 like BRONFAY. 2/R11 2nd Lieut on leave. Section parades, headquarters and stoppages. Signallers practised use of the lamp 33er. Camp cleared up. (Refuse pits dug. Transport & lines cleaned and drawn dry.) Lieut Hyslop and 1 O.R. returned from leave. O.C. Company and two other officers visited 119th Infantry Bn Company 40th Division hqs in MAURÉPAS RAVINE visited by RANCOURT transport officer.	no appx
	3rd		Inspection parades. Rifles, gas helmets, box respirators, emergency rations, full dressings and identity discs inspected. Latrine pits to be cleaned up. Camp and transport linesduring the day. 1 O.R. returned from Signalling course. Signallers practised semaphore during morning.	YCL

Army Form C. 2118.

WAR DIARY
or
INTELLIGENCE SUMMARY

(Erase heading not required.)

Place	Date	Hour	Summary of Events and Information	Remarks and references to Appendices
CAMP 16 BROMFAY FARM	Jan 4th		Section parades, mechanism, stoppages, and lecture on individual fire. Signallers practised on buzzer. Rifles, gases and box respirators inspected. Kit rifled.	nil.
	5th		Section parades. Mechanism and stoppages. Inspection of rifles, gas helmets, box respirators, full dressings, emergency rations and identity discs. Semaphore drill for signallers. Fatigue parties cleaning up camp and transport lines and fetching wood. 1 officer and 1 n.r. to Divisional Chief 3. O.R. to Gas Course.	nil.
	6th		Section parades. Mechanism, stoppages and indication and recognition of targets. Gas drill. Semaphore buzzer semaphore. Fatigue parties cleaned up camp & transport lines and filled wood. Transport lines inspected by G.O.C.	nil.
	7th		Section parades. Fitting of equipment, rifle inspection, indication and recognition of targets. Church parade in hut ntd 1st Worcestershire Regt.	nil.
	8th		Section parades. Rifle inspection. Instruction and recognition of targets. Semaphore and house practice for signallers. Usual fatigue parties.	nil.

Army Form C. 2118.

WAR DIARY
or
INTELLIGENCE SUMMARY

(Erase heading not required.)

Instructions regarding War Diaries and Intelligence Summaries are contained in F. S. Regs., Part II. and the Staff Manual respectively. Title Pages will be prepared in manuscript.

Place	Date	Hour	Summary of Events and Information	Remarks and references to Appendices
CAMP 16 BRONFAY FARM	9th		Section parades, lectures & stoppages. Rifle inspection, feet rubbed & leathers packed. 3 O.R. returned from Anti-Gas Course.	/ICL
	10th		2 O.R. returned from leave. Lorry loaded at 8 A.M. Company paraded at 10.45 A.M. and marched to SAILLY-LE-SEC via BRAY and BEL-AIR Station.	/ICL
SAILLY-LE-SEC	11th		Lorry loaded at 6 A.M. Company paraded at 6.15 A.M. and marched to MERICOURT L'ABBÉ station where it entrained. Transport marched to ST SAUVEUR under Lt Higham. Train went through CORBIE & AMIENS to DIGEMONT. Company marched to billets in EPAUMESNIL.	/ICL
EPAUMESNIL	12th		Section parades 10.30 A.M. Rifle inspection. Greatcoats, kit etc cleaned up & Billets swept out. Transport marched from ST SAUVEUR to EPAUMESNIL.	/ICL

WAR DIARY
or
INTELLIGENCE SUMMARY

(Erase heading not required.)

Army Form C. 2118.

Place	Date	Hour	Summary of Events and Information	Remarks and references to Appendices
FROMESNIL	13TH		Transport taken over by Lieut R.M. Hale. Lieut R.B. Bonner attached to Staff as Lieut. F.G. Higham took over as 1st section. Route march through ST. MAULVIS & CAMPSART. Commanding Officer's lecture at Ride. H.Q. 1 O.R. returned from Bayonet fighting Course.	yes.
	14TH		Section parades. Cleaning up Limbers wanted. Rifle inspection. Re-skirmishing practised. Spare hit fitted to drum at BELLOY-ST-LEONARD. Cpl. Tomlinson who is a nursery train awarded the Military Medal was awarded the Distinguished Conduct Medal.	nil.
	15TH		Running drill. Company parade for gun drill, gun drill, transport preparing for inspection. Lt. Inchenson & officers Ruther, granet & oliver Lt. Cunningham & 2 O.R. proceed on leave to absence to United Kingdom. Physical drill. Range, grouping practices were fired. Revolver practise. Lecture in afternoon "Indirect and light firing." Inspection of rifles, emergency rations, p's helmets and field dressings. transport preparing for inspection.	yes.
	16TH			yes.
	17TH		Running drill. Lecture. Range boards in attack and in defence. Semaphore drill mechanism in afternoon. Limbers packed ready for inspection.	yes.
	18TH		Physical drill. Company cleaning up for inspection. Brigade transport inspected by Brigade Commander on main OISEMONT - ARGUEL Road	yes.

Army Form C. 2118.

WAR DIARY
or
INTELLIGENCE SUMMARY
(Erase heading not required.)

Place	Date	Hour	Summary of Events and Information	Remarks and references to Appendices
EPAUMESNIL	18th Jan (contd)	2 p.m.	Company marched to VERGIES in afternoon for inspection of brigade by Brigade Commander.	WCL.
	19th		Running drill. SS 4-44 Army Act read out. Instruction in preparing message cards and semaphore. Inspection of gas helmets, emergency rations and field dressings. Revolver practice in afternoon. Baths for Hdqrs and Nos 1 & 2 sections. All horses inspected by A.D.V.S. Conference at Bde Hdqrs. WOIREL. Major Lewis lectured at Divisional School on "Tactical Employment of Machine Guns and Lewis Guns." 2 O.R. returned from leave.	WCL.
	20th		Physical drill. Range. Machine gun practices and revolver practices were fired. Bombing practice. Spare kit dumped at BELLOY ST LEONARD. Rifle inspection. Medical inspection. Baths for nos. 3 & 4 sections and transport. Arm drill and musketry in afternoon. Limbers packed. 1 O.R. returned from leave.	WCL.
	21st		Transport marched to starting point at Cross Roads near ALLERY on main DISEMONT-AIRAINES Rd. Marched through AIRAINES, SOUES (where horses were watered and fed), CAMP to CAMP 13 near SALLY LAURETTE PICQUIGNY, BREILLY to billets in AILLY-SUR-SOMME. Inspection parades.	WCL.

Army Form C. 2118.

WAR DIARY
or
INTELLIGENCE SUMMARY
(Erase heading not required.)

Instructions regarding War Diaries and Intelligence Summaries are contained in F.S. Regs., Part II. and the Staff Manual respectively. Title Pages will be prepared in manuscript.

Place	Date	Hour	Summary of Events and Information	Remarks and references to Appendices
EPAUMESNIL	Jan 22nd		Company marched to OISEMONT where it entrained. Detrained at EDGEHILL STATION near BERNANCOURT and marched to CAMP 12 near SAILLY LAURETTE. Extra Kit taken from EPAUMESNIL to OISEMONT by lorry and also from EDGEHILL to CAMP 12. Transport marched from AILLY SUR SOMME through DREUIL, AMIENS, DAOURS (where horses were watered and fed), CORBIE, to CAMP 12.	YCh
CAMP 12 near SAILLY LAURETTE	23rd		Section parades. Limbers unpacked. Guns and gun pit cleaned. Gas helmets and box respirators inspected. Transport took over lines from 2nd Batt. Duke of Wellington's Regt. IV Div. 2 O.R. proceeded on leave.	YCh
	24th		Physical drill. Section parades. Rifle inspection. Rifle & squad drill. Lecture to N.C.O.'s on Discipline by O.C. Company.	YCh
	25th		O.C. Company visited trenches. Company paraded 7.30 A.M. and marched to starting point on main BRAY - CORBIE Rd. Bde group marched through BRAY and SUZANNE to CAMP 17. 1 O.R. returned from leave.	YCh
CAMP 17.	26th		Moved from Camp 17 at 10 a.m. to ANGOSTURA. Halted here ½ hour; from thence on to the positions in the Line. Nos. 1. 5. 6. 7. 8. guns in front positions. Nos. 2. 3. 4 and 9 guns in intermediate line Nos. 10 and 12 A.A. at ANDOVER PLACE.	YCh

WAR DIARY
or
INTELLIGENCE SUMMARY

(Erase heading not required.)

Army Form C. 2118.

Place	Date	Hour	Summary of Events and Information	Remarks and references to Appendices
TRENCHES	JAN 26	—	Nos 11, 13, 14, 15, 16 Guns & Brigade H.Q. at ANGOSTURA under Lt BEECHMAN. Relief complete 7.15 pm. O.C. By had visited all guns 8pm.	MCh
"	27th	—	Fine day. Frost still holding. O.C. Company visited trenches in morning and evening, also AN GOS TU RA in afternoon. Enemy shelled hain Rd, BAPAUME-BETHUNE Rd intermittently during the night. This road was mined on west side (N 300 west gun position (REBECCA). 2 Lt SULLY returned from leave.	MCh
"	29th	—	Frost still holding. O.C. Company visited all forward Guns in the evening. Wiring along road carried on: also in front of REBECCA GUN. Rations, water etc, brought up by pack animals for first time.	MCh

Army Form C. 2118.

WAR DIARY
or
INTELLIGENCE SUMMARY
(Erase heading not required.)

Instructions regarding War Diaries and Intelligence Summaries are contained in F. S. Regs., Part II. and the Staff Manual respectively. Title Pages will be prepared in manuscript.

Place	Date	Hour	Summary of Events and Information	Remarks and references to Appendices
TRENCHES	29th	—	Front still holding. 5 cals. French line carried up to No. 2 Section's Sept. O.C. Company visits Trenches at 6 pm also ANGOSTURA twice during the day. About 7 pm. Major Alan, S.O.S. Some Artillery activity on both Sides resulted	JCL.
"	30th		O.C. Company & 2nd Lt. Bally, SULLY and 2 Sergeants attend A.A. lecture at Camp "9" Rt CURLU. Relief takes place. Forward Positions : Nos. 2.3.4.9.10. Guns Intermediate line No.5. 13.14.15.16. Guns. A.A. ANDOVER Pt. No.5. 11.12. GUNS. ANGOSTURA Nos. 1.5.6.7.8. GUNS Relief complete by 7.30pm.	JCL.
"	31st		Front quiet still holding. O.C. Company visited all forward guns. Enemy intermittently shelled ANDOVER PLACE with 4.2" shells	JCL.

Sgd. F.J.C. Lewis Major

Vol 14

War Diary
of
24th Machine Gun Company
for
February 1917
by
Major F E C Lewis

To:- D.A.G.
BASE

Herewith - War Diary for the month of February 1917.

F.P.C. Neire Major
Comdg 24th M.G. Coy

2/3/17

WAR DIARY or INTELLIGENCE SUMMARY

Army Form C. 2118.

Place	Date	Hour	Summary of Events and Information	Remarks and references to Appendices
TRENCHES.	Feb 1st		Front still holding. O.C. Coy accompanied by 2nd Lieut JOLLY & 2 Sgts went to A.A. Assumption. Watch was prepared. O.C. Coy reconnoitered front positions with G.O.C. 25th Inf. Bn. Front still holding. Above-named officers & men attend P.A.A. demonstration at	
	2nd		Aire Drome on BRAY - MEAULTE RD. O.C. COY, Lts WALKINGTON & PIKE visit lines during the evening. 2nd Lt PIKE having returned from 8th Divn General Course. Lt A.D. CUMMING returns from leave. Relief took place. Complete by 7.15 am. Distribution of guns as follows:-	
	3rd		(A) FORWARD POSITIONS Nos 13.14.15.16. - (B) BAPAUME RD No 7.8.(C) INTERMEDIATE LINE Nos 5. 6. 9. 12. (D) A.A. ANDOVER PLACE 10. 11. (E) ANGOSTURA No 1.2.3.4. O.C. Coy reconnoitres ground for "A.A." position to cover Front line & spurs - Front commences intense cold. Enemy shelled ANDOVER PLACE and ridge on the right during morning. Front still holding O.C. Coy visited guns in evening.	
	4th		Front continues. Lecture in Small Box Respirator cancelled.	
	5th		Front still holding. Relief taken place. Mooring and Distribution of guns:-	
	6th		FORWARD POSITIONS Nos 9.10.11.12. BAPAUME RD Nos 5.6. No 4 gun. Relief complete by 7.30 a.m.	
	7th		ANGOSTURA Nos 13.15.16. 2.5.14.13. 3rd Area No 4 gun. Relief complete by 7.30 a.m. Intermediate line 1.2.3.14. O.C. 2/5th M.G. Coy + O.C. Coy views No 4 gun in position at H.Q. Supplies Coy Royal Rn 2.5th Inf. Bn. Front is the intention on "B" front & in the right of in the right of 11.15 a.m.	
	8th	6 am	Artillery activity on the right became intermittent throughout the day. Officer 9/10 the M.G. Coy met Lt Colonel Major LONG of 10th M.R.S. Coy was shown various lines of O.C Coy. 6 gun was placed at 2/5th Inf Bn Area. No 9 team. No shelter -	

Army Form C. 2118.

WAR DIARY
or
INTELLIGENCE SUMMARY

(Erase heading not required.)

Instructions regarding War Diaries and Intelligence Summaries are contained in F. S. Regs., Part II. and the Staff Manual respectively. Title Pages will be prepared in manuscript.

Place	Date	Hour	Summary of Events and Information	Remarks and references to Appendices
Tincourt. (BOUCHAVESNES)	Feb. 10th		No. C.O.Y. upon arrival in the line by No 10 th M.G. Coy. Relief completed by 6.15 p.m. The C.O.Y. marched to Camp No 117 arriving about 11.30 p.m.	W/S
Camp 117 } Camp 12 }	11.2.	4 am	No 2 Section arrived in camp from trenches. Transport moves to Camp 112 (A Lines) detraining at 11 a.m. The C.O.Y. moved up at 12 Noon arriving at Camp 12 (B Lines) at 1.15 p.m. Conference of all officers by the Brigadier at SAILLY LAURETTE at 4 p.m.	W/S

WAR DIARY
or
INTELLIGENCE SUMMARY

(Erase heading not required.)

Army Form C. 2118.

Place	Date	Hour	Summary of Events and Information	Remarks and references to Appendices
CAMP 12. (N⁰. 1 PIPPLY)	Feb. 12th	10 AM	Section Parade. Cleaning of gear - kit scrubbing & equipment etc. C⁰y parties engaged in their cooking. Starting with N⁰.1 section. Afternoon - State Parade. The following postings took effect:- Lt BEECHMAN attd to C⁰y H⁰, LT HIGHAM to N⁰2 section, 2/Lt SULLY N⁰3 platoon. 2/Lt WARRINGTON became O.C. N⁰4 section. 13 P. Bell has been posted from 10th M.G.C⁰y at 5th Brigade in exchange for thos left by this C⁰y to the Div.	
Feb. 13th			4 O.R.s return from leave. O.C. C⁰y inspects all deport dugouts (tunnels & rifles).	
		7.30-8	Physical Training. 10-12 Cleaning.	
		2-3 P.M.	Drill Parade for fatigues between camps. 6.30 2/Lt PILL & 2/Lt WARRINGTON attend lecture on "CONTACT PATROL WORK at SAILLY LAURETTE. C⁰y proceed. Seven cars conditions.	
Feb. 14th	7.30		Physical Drill. 10-11 a.m. Gun Drill, O.C. C⁰y inspected all tele-boxes. 11 a.m - 12 noon Trouble Zis & Night Firing (practice). Afternoon - Gun-drill. 2/Lt SULLY, 2/Lt PILL & 2/Lt O.R. is (prone) in flat artillery course with P⁴ fothery at SOZANNE	
Feb.15th	2 a.m.		O.C. C⁰y recom[?] fainted by Major LACEY O.C. 140th M.C. C⁰y proceeded to recce routes in elim. No. BOUCHAVESNES returning at 6 P.M.	
		7.30	Physical training. 10 am - 12 noon Parade & Baths for whole C⁰y at Camp 12. Visit by Lt Col. CLARKE Corps M.C. Officer.	
		2-3 P.M.	Rifle drill. 2/Lt C.B.A. CAMPBELL, temporarily in charge of transport, posted back to N⁰.1 section.	
Feb.16th			3 O.R.'s to hospital.	
		7.30.	Parade. Physical Training. Bayonet Parade. 11-12 noon Battalion by Sections & Organization. Sun drill. Class 9 pupils when commenced under Cpl KING to learn O.R's recently joined. 2-3 P.M. Field Parade.	

Army Form C. 2118.

WAR DIARY
or
INTELLIGENCE SUMMARY
(Erase heading not required.)

Instructions regarding War Diaries and Intelligence Summaries are contained in F. S. Regs., Part II. and the Staff Manual respectively. Title Pages will be prepared in manuscript.

Place	Date	Hour	Summary of Events and Information	Remarks and references to Appendices
CAMP 12 (nr CHIPILLY)	Feb 17th	7.30am	9am Physical Training. 10–11am Boot-filling. 11am–12 Noon Mechanism 2–3pm Bomb-throwing. General NIVELLE accompanied by F.M. Commander-in-chief visited IV Army Area	J/B.
"	18th		4 O.R's from hospital. Inspection Parade 10.30am. At Noon there was a Coy E Church Parade conducted by Rev. Millcar – at Coy H.Q. There was also a Service for R.C.'s at CHIPILLY.	J/B.
"	19th	7:30am	Physical Training 10–11am Boot-fitting pm 11–15–12.15 – Boot-filling & stripping (7 mens) – Cpl KING took an elementary class of Instruction. 4.45 PM. Major Fiery with auxiliary seeing marks in rear W of CAMP 12. 2 O.A.V SULLY, 2 Lt G.C.R. PILL & 2 O.R.s return from short	J/B. 2/Lt W. SEDDON join. Coy
"	20th	7.30am	artillery course at SUZANNE. 2/Lt W. SEDDON join Coy from GRANTHAM. Physical Training. 10–11am Dripping. 11.15–12.15 Mechanism. 2–3 pm stripping. 2/Lt W. SEDDON 14 Reinforcements posted to No 4 Section.	C/R. J/B.
CAMP 12 SUZANNE	21st	8am	17 BEECHAM proceed to hinder to reconnoitre position in MARRIERE WOOD with a view to 2/14 T.S. Coy firing cooperation in support of a H.G. Barrage to an attack to be made by 19 & Inf Bde (33rd Divn) on morning 23/2/17. There was no casualties. Coy move off from Camp 12 to SUZANNE arriving 2.30pm. Coy accommodate in huts. 10R. 1 hosp.	J/B.
"		10.30		
SUZANNE CAMP 17	22nd	9am	Breakfasts. 11 am Inspection Parade. 2.30 PM. Coy move to CAMP 17. Their new post. Reduction of transport facilities. 1 O.R. to hospital.	J/B.
CAMP 17	23rd	8am	5 O.R. Reinforcements (including 3 ols members of Coy & a cook there). Breakfasts.	Ref: 8th Div. War. G.O. 784.

J.B.C. Davis Major
Cmdg. 243 M.Gun Company
1.3.17

WAR DIARY
or
INTELLIGENCE SUMMARY

(Erase heading not required.)

Army Form C. 2118.

Place	Date	Hour	Summary of Events and Information	Remarks and references to Appendices
Camp 17 nr SUZANNE	Feb 24		O.C. Coy visits brickworks returning at 6 P.M. 2nd Lt Lef, Brit. fails to furnish return of men and not full evening until 9.30 am, under Coy arrangement. Remains to hand to him return. Gentlemen of men inspire inability of Corpl.	M.
LANGTON B^ks	25		O.C. Coy visits brickworks at 10 am returning at 6.30. Party of 30, including Recruits, en. my fum. inspired & Kit Sh. to LANGTON BARRACKS leaving men 2nd Lt. CAMPBELL at 11.15 am and arriving at 4.30. Parade via LITTLE DALE DUMP. Run. take point to LOCK BARRACKS Lgr. Ry was used.	M.
	26		O.C. Coy visits brickworks party at 10.45 am. Walk one man - brickworks. Brew; made shelters in BOUCHAVESNES area -- Inspected funds for remaining men at CAMP 17 - morning. Afternoon, went on Transport lines. 3 O.Rs. praid. 10 R. to hospital. 1 O.R. from hospital.	M.
	27		O.C. Coy visits brickers at 10 am - returning at 6 p.m. to inspect construction of gun position site. Fn. recovering men 70.07 Inspection parade 10 am - 11 N.	M.
	28		Lt BEECHMAN visits brickers. Work on disable gun - position. Frose very quiet. Inspection parade. Arms drill fn. remainder of Coy. morning. Work at Kempart Road Cais afternoon.	M.

Vol 15

War Diary of
24th Machine Gun Company
by
Major F.E.C Lewis
for the month of
March 1917

Army Form C. 2118.

WAR DIARY
or
INTELLIGENCE SUMMARY

(Erase heading not required.)

Instructions regarding War Diaries and Intelligence Summaries are contained in F.S. Regs., Part II. and the Staff Manual respectively. Title Pages will be prepared in manuscript.

Place	Date	Hour	Summary of Events and Information	Remarks and references to Appendices
CAMP 17. (N⁰ SUZANNE) & LANGTON BARRACKS (N⁰ BOUCHAVESNES)	March 1st	10 a.m.	O.C. Coy orders kinder returning at 5 P.M. Search for fur-jerkins was completed. Inspection passed & rifles rifle for the remainder of the Coy at CAMP 17. 1 O.R. from H.Q.	J/B
	March 2nd	8 a.m.	Breakfast. Kit stored at Camp 17. The following unmasked place in the afternoon.	J/B P. Doris G. 12/190.
LANGTON BARRACKS		2 P.M.	2 LT CAMPBELL proceeded with advance to LANGTON BARKS. Relieving with him 19 O.R. for kinder.	
		3 P.M.	8 guns (2 per section) were placed in having position. O.C. Coy accompanied by LT BEECHAM arrived at LANGTON BARKS from SUZANNE & took up his position for the night after inspecting 145 guns which were in position. Coy Transport arrived at 4 P.M. & wood, stone, transport stores were taken on. 1 Mr. from H.Q.	J/B
	3rd	5 A.M.	O.C. Coy took up his position on slope S. of BOUCHAVESNES in BOUCH — QUARRY FM RD, ADVANCED COY HQ. 16 guns in Barrage position disposed as follows:— LT JOLLY (4 guns) N⁰ 1 section QUARRY.	
”		2 P.M.		"
		3 A.M.	LT HIGHAM N⁰ 2 section (4 guns) LT CUMMING N⁰ 2 section in position (4 guns) the Sunken road S. of BOUCH. 2 LT WALKINGTON N⁰ 4 section (4 guns) slightly E. of latter point. All arrangements were continued by 6 P.M.	P. L⁰ Worc. N⁰ 162 J/B P. L⁰ Div. G. 12/117.
		4 P.M.	O.C. Coy checked laying of all guns in person. 2 LT CAMPBELL supervised and watched all at 13th H.Q. ALDERSHOT at 3 P.M. & 9 P.M. 2 O.R. from host. 10.R. to host.	
”	4th	5.15 a.m.	At 5.15 hours an attack was carried out by 2nd & & 2.5th Inf. Bdes 12. & N.E. of BOUCHAVESNES. with a view to attaining MOISLAINS & BOUCH. Gulley & RANCOURT areas. The ultimate object of the 24th Inf. Bde was FRITZ TRENCH. The 18th WORC. R. occupied the spur of the attacking front & the 2 NORTHR. R. left. There were separate arrangements for support by the Division or our Reinfts. inducing the attack. Contact aeroplanes, moving & fires artillery barrage etc. The rifles of planes were notified as regards Yale which was followed from Feb. 27th also in their support. Sp. provision open St. for emergencies of the 50th Division of the 19th M.G. Barrage was also supplying an elevation for the guns increased. Two sects. from M.G. Coys of the Division & the 120th M.G. Coy. formed a barrage on the front & flanks of the attack.	J/B 2.4th B.M. O.O. 151. J/B G. 12/184.

WAR DIARY
INTELLIGENCE SUMMARY

Army Form C. 2118.

Place	Date	Hour	Summary of Events and Information	Remarks and references to Appendices
LONDON BARRACKS	March 4.3.17	5.15 a.m.	The 2&W M.G. Coy fired a barrage between BREMEN TR. & GERMAN WOOD TR. one section (N.21) delivering its fire on the right of MT.B.M. front. At 5.20 a.m. 6 all guns opened fire till 5.40 + 10 firing at the rate of 125 a. per minute + 40. It was laid down that after this firing all guns should then fire 10 minutes at the rate of 125 per minute when silent. The signal for M.G. fire only was I Green Parachute Very Light repeated till fire should be ceased. 2/Lt CAMPBELL was in charge of O.P. at C.15.c. central where to contact Batm. signals. He was assisted by 3 signallers. Fire was found necessary to the above arrangements all the guns firing well.	G 12/52 Appendix III
		11 a.m.	Lt F.S. BEECHAM recommended to bar-position in MAYFLOWER TRENCH (S. of Quarry) with a view to a relief taking place in the evening, but this was cancelled by the Division. 2 O.R. ✗ off wounded.	G 12/117
	5th	8.15 a.m.	The above took place 8 gun relieving a Division M.G. of firing the 232 M.G. Coy. Lt SEDDON was in charge of 2 guns from each section. From 9 Am. 2.1 Feb. also position Mayflower in position the Division remained unaltered. TR. C.2. c.6. 9.5r.8°.	G 12/126
		4 p.m. 6.55 p.m.	Sever bombardment by our artillery. The signal for M.G. barrage was given by his infantry in front & acted upon. Intermittent firing was carried out during the night which the 232 M.G. Coy were known is fire plan where reinforcements were and I return being led by Mayflower. 1 O.R. to hosp. 3 O.R. off wounded.	
	6th	6 am. 5.3.17 6 am. 6.3.17	N° wound field 14,000. The enemy trenches were heavy from 11 am. Lt A.D. CUMMING was killed by shell fire. Later in position cutting wire with fire of Lewis cable + at 11 am Lt A.D. CUMMING was killed by shell fire. 3 O.R. of N° 3 Section Pts McMANUS, NEWBY & KENT were killed by the same shell. Later in the day Pts WILLOUGHBY N°2 Section was wounded in the back & CROUSBY of Western Section hospital seven shell-shock. O.C. Coy inside B.H.R.	1 officer killed
		11 am	in the afternoon	

WAR DIARY
or
INTELLIGENCE SUMMARY

Army Form C. 2118.

Place	Date	Hour	Summary of Events and Information	Remarks and references to Appendices
(LONDON BARRACKS) TRENCHES	March 6/7/17		During the night 6/7th 2nd Lieut Fir was carried out on the previous night 14,500r being fired. 1 O.R. to hosp. - 10R. off duty wh., 1 off. + 3 O.R. killed 2 M.R. wounded.	G.12/126 etc. ditto. J.M.
		7 a.m.	A/T ABERCROMBIE maintained positions in the AANCOURT area - others were to relieving 121st M.G. Coy.	
"			L. Coy of 11th + positions of the 231st M.G. Coy.	Ly. W. Ing. M.R. B.M. 3.22 —
		2 P.M.	Burial of 2/Lt CUNNING + 3 O.R. at LONGTON BARRACKS. 2/Lt JULLY + 2/Lt WALKINGTON relieved 23rd M.G. Coy with 4 pun fired at the Flanding position 2/Lt JULLY RUPERT + ROSALIND. Their two positions were taken by D.C. Coy & + WARRINGTON frames two gun at ROSE!. This wing was complete by 9 P.M. The D.E. Coy under the guns in	
		9 P.M.	completion of relief.	Sele dies. G.12/126
		9.30 P.M.	The enemy fired fair shells in the neighborhood of LONGTON Bks.	J.M.
"	8th		No rounds fired in enemy lines night 7/8th Nr. 10,520 R. The enemy still firmed the fr position on the ridge S. of BOUCHAVESNES. The enemy position were (weak) the disposition of the guns being as follows. All the forage positions were LINK LUCY + ROSALIND. No 1 position guns at LENA. M.O. 1.2.3.4. in the ANDOVER VALLEY (CORPSLINE). " 2 " " " " 3 guns in reserve at LONGTON BARRACKS from at LUCY. " 3 " " " " 2 guns at ROSE! 2 guns A.A. position ANDOVER VALLEY. " 4 " " " " 9 P.M. O.C. Coy took up his quarters Main BETHUNE —	
TRENCHES (LAZARUS)		9 a.m.	This relief was completed by 9 P.M. PERONNE Rd in REBECCA (LAZARUS). During the period 4th — 8th incl, 106,000 r. were fired by the Coy.	

WAR DIARY
or
INTELLIGENCE SUMMARY

(Erase heading not required.)

Army Form C. 2118.

Place	Date	Hour	Summary of Events and Information	Remarks and references to Appendices
TRENCHES	MARCH 9th	2.30 P.M.	O.C. Coy took up his H.Q. at LANGTON BARRACKS.	J.B.
"		5.30 P.M.	O.C. Coy visited the guns. There was heavy shelling in the RANCOURT area especially in the neighbourhood of ARTHURS SEAT. 6 P.M. – 10 P.M. 1 O.R. to hosp.	J.B.
"	10th		During the morning the enemy searched the road with MG position on the Mt. Mr. S.O.7. BOUCHAVESNES with gun of heavy calibre. An intermittent whiz. bang. fire continued by 5 P.M. 1 O.R. to hosp.	J.B.
"	11th	10.30 a.m.	Owing to a report that the Enemy was making a advance in the direction of the station occupied by the 2 i/c. B.E., all arms "Stood-to" from 10.30 a.m. until 7 p.m. M Enemy aeroplanes showed great aerial activity owing to the very auspicious weather.	J.B.
"		1 P.M.	An enemy aeroplane descended in flames behind our lines. Shot down to LANGTON B.M.R in reserve.	
"		10.30 P.M.	23rd M.G. Coy retain the fire on RUPERT which was withdrawn to LANGTON B.M.R. Troops MOUTAINS WOOD.	
"			6,000 x fired during night 11th/12th. Troops MOUTAINS WOOD.	
"	12th	12 N.	The situation was the normal. Usual retook on either side. O.C. Coy visited the guns.	J.B.
			2. In the afternoon an interesting exhibit took place when M.Co visited returning No.2 Section on the ground gained from Transport 9th Coy H.Q. when in reserve.	
		5 P.M.	C.S.M. arrived from TroU.S.WOOD. 5000 x fired night 12th/13th Troops MOUTAINS WOOD. L.T. WATKINGTH & 1 N.C.O. examined an A.A. crew at "P" Battery SUZANNE. 2 O'Rsk hosp. 1 O.R. from hosp.	

Army Form C. 2118.

WAR DIARY
or
INTELLIGENCE SUMMARY
(Erase heading not required.)

Place	Date	Hour	Summary of Events and Information	Remarks and references to Appendices
TRENCHES. (LAMBETH BRKS)	MARCH 13th	10.30 am	Lt BECKMAN visited bayonet fire from ROSE I to COY HQ from ROSE I to COY HQ in reserve.	T/B
		6 P.M.	1 O.R. left strength. O.C. COY visited the firing.	T/B
"	14th		O.C. COY visited the firing. The enemy shewn little activity. A Light Trench Mortar fired 6 shots this being its the first. Change of clothing issued to transport during the day.	T/B
			2nd Lt H.E. COY came under the command of the 2nd Lt Reg B.I.	
"	15th	10 am	2 New places N.E. of BOUCH (C.14.B.3.5.) in position selected by O.C. COY to command BOIS CHAVESNES valley & to carry out indirect fire.	T/B
		2 P.M.	O.C. COY visited the firing.	
		3 P.M.	Fire of our aeroplanes prevented an A.A. position in ANDOVER valley owing to superior altitude.	T/B
"	16th		3 O.R.s to hosp. 1 O.R. from hosp. 1 P.R. Off strength. Enemy plane fell S.E. of BOUCH! & another nr ROSE 1. Envelopes aired rebuilt, one of our planes fell S.E. of BOUCH! & another nr ROSE 1.	T/B
		1 A.M.	COY HQ shifted to BETHUNE RD near REBECCA DUMP & return from reserve.	
		4 P.M.	G.t. LANGTON BARRACKS.	
			The enemy commenced a retirement.	
"	17th		Enemy now shews no signs of activity.	T/B
		10 am	O.C. COY visited the firing.	
"	18th	5 P.M.	Lt MEEHAM & 2nd Lt CAMPBELL left England to join a M.G. course at G.H.Q. M.G. School. O.C. COY accompanied by Lt SIVEY visited MOISLAINS letter being the first winner of the 2nd B.N. to reach that point, starting at 9.30 a.m. An object was to reconnoitre of positions with a view to holding our same there.	T/B
			1 O.R. to hosp.	

Army Form C. 2118.

WAR DIARY
or
INTELLIGENCE SUMMARY
(Erase heading not required.)

Instructions regarding War Diaries and Intelligence Summaries are contained in F.S. Regs., Part II. and the Staff Manual respectively. Title Pages will be prepared in manuscript.

Place	Date	Hour	Summary of Events and Information	Remarks and references to Appendices
TRENCHES	MARCH 19th	11:30 am	O.C. Coy again reconnoitred forward area. The front of this Coy. moved to the "Fisherieshütte" line & from retiring 23rd M.G. Coy to similar No. 2 & M.G. Coy. C.O.Y H.Q. were moved to MARRIÈRE WOOD. The relief was complete by 5 P.M. 1 O.R. to Hosp.	J.N.
"	20th		2 it. wounded. O.C. Coy accompanied by Lt Neale visited his forward area. There was no sign of the enemy opposite B.Q. vicinity W of road PERONNE-ALIECOURT. Men in "line" issued with clean pair of socks. 2 O.Rs from Coy.	J.N.
"	21st	6:30 am	O.C. Coy accompanied by 2nd Lt Suvly reconnoitred with a view to taking up position in the defence of the new line N.E. of MOISLAINS. Working party found escort 2Lt Mill & Lt Neddon for road repairs in town.	J.N.
"	22nd	1:30 PM 9 am	B.O.C.H. - MOISLAINS Rd. returning at 6 P.M. B.O. Coy accompanied by 2Lt Pike visited forward area to reconnoitre for positions for defence of the line & resistance & to the outpost line.	J.N. G.S. - 13th G. 619.-
"	"	12:30 P.M.	Working party of 40 available men, (escort for work on roads, under 2Lt Suvly & Lt Neddon returning at 7 A.M. 2 Lt. Malkington + 1 N.C.O refused 2nd Coy H.Q. from A.A. Group at "P" failing SUZANNE.	J.N.
"	23rd	1 P.M.	O.C. Coy accompanied by Lt Neale visited the forward area. 2 O.R. to hosp. 6 O.R. joined.	J.N.

Army Form C. 2118.

WAR DIARY
or
INTELLIGENCE SUMMARY

(Erase heading not required.)

Place	Date	Hour	Summary of Events and Information	Remarks and references to Appendices
(MARRIERE WOOD) TRENCHES.	March 24th	10 am 12.30 p.m.	Totally known at Coy H.Q. Working party formed under Lt Sully for road repair. (BOUCH:- MOISLAINS RD) returning at 6 p.m.	J/S.
MOISLAINS (BILLETS).	25th		The Coy moved to MOISLAINS. Coy TRANSPORT moved off from point at Junction of main BETHUNE & HIGH ST. BOUCH: at 11 am. All avail. wte men employed. The usual working party on completion they moved into billets at MOISLAINS arriving at 6.30 P.M. Coy Transport moved from Y. WOOD to CLERY.	J/S.
"	26th		Morning Inspection parade, cleaning of gas kits etc. cleaning of billets. In the afternoon. No 1 section under Lt Sully occupied A.A. position near the MANANCOURT CANAL & S.W. of VAUX WOOD. ½ No 2 section (No. 5 & 6 guns) occupied A.A. position in OPERA & MIDINITES TR.	J/S.
"	27th		Transport moved from CLERY to MOISLAINS. A working party to work on the roads. 2 O.R. from hosp.	J/S.
"	28th		Coy stores were removed from CAMP 17. The usual working party was employed in the morning. 2 O.R. from hosp.	J/S.
"	29th		7.15 - 8 am cleaning of equipment etc. At 9.15 Coy paraded for G.O.C. inspection. Parade 7.15 - 8 am cleaning of equipment etc. At 9.15 Coy paraded for G.O.C. inspection. 10 am 2 p.m. 2.15 p.m.	Bn's HOR flew at Coy H.Q. at 10 am. Working party formed under Lt WILKINSON to work on roads. Lt. Coy area formed by Lt Sully reconnected forward area. 1 O.R. to hosp.	J/S.

2449 Wt. W14957/M90 750,000 1/16 J.B.C. & A. Forms/C.2118/12.

Army Form C. 2118.

WAR DIARY
or
INTELLIGENCE SUMMARY
(Erase heading not required.)

Instructions regarding War Diaries and Intelligence Summaries are contained in F. S. Regs., Part II. and the Staff Manual respectively. Title Pages will be prepared in manuscript.

Place	Date	Hour	Summary of Events and Information	Remarks and references to Appendices
MOISLAINS	MARCH 30.	10.15 am	Professional Section - praises; cleaning of gun - kit: for this purpose the teams were practised in the handling of the German M.G. care being in effect to the M.G. Magazine. Winter was fairly fall. Coy was allowed to turn tellets without permission.	F/B
		2 PM	Coy fell in in mass of the Coy was prepared to leave at 1/2 an hour's notice to support an attack.	
		4 PM.	After 4 PM. the Coy was prepared to leave at 1/2 an hour's notice to support an attack. Nothing issued.	F/B
"	31st	12.15 am	An enemy aeroplane fired on HOISLAINS putting 7 bombs; returned shortly after dropping new ones. Our own Lewis fire the enemy machine was actually invisible.	
		9.30	Cleaning of guns. Kit etc. Rehearsan. O.C. Coy accompanied by Lt. MEALE & 2/Lt G.O.R.PILL reconnoitred positions to be taken on Johnny Day. They returned at 6 PM.	
		1.45 PM	from the 23rd M.G. Coy in the Johnny Day They returned at 6 PM	
		3 PM.	2 Teams No.1 Section (LIDDLE) being withdrawn from their original A.A. positions, occupied A.A. positions in MOISLAINS vid Coy H.Q.	

J.E.C. Kerr Major
and/24th M.G.C.

31.3.17

From O.C. 24th N.G. Co?
To. D.A.G. Base.

Herewith copy War Diary Month
of April 1917.

1.5.17.

[signature]
Lt.
for O.C. 24th N.G. Co?

24 M.G. Coy
Vol 16

WAR DIARY
or
INTELLIGENCE SUMMARY

Army Form C. 2118.

(Erase heading not required.)

Place	Date	Hour	Summary of Events and Information	Remarks and references to Appendices
LIERAMONT.	APRIL 1st	9.10am	The Coy moved from MOISLAINS to LIERAMONT, arriving at 10.45 am. The 23rd M.G. Coy was relieved in the line, the following being the Disposition of the guns:—	24th Inf. B.M. O. 148. J.B.
			No.1 Section. LT SULLY. 1 gun A.A. Stationed at Coy H.Q. LIERAMONT. 2 guns in cemetery N.E. of LIERAMONT. 1 gun at factory S. of LIERAMONT.	
			No.2 Section. 2nd LT SEDDON. 2 guns LIERAMONT — SOREL Rd.	
			1 gun 500x S.E. NURLU WOOD. 1 gun nr HEUDECOURT — SOREL Rd.	
			No.3 Section. 2nd LT. 4 guns BUYENCOURT Subsidiary 1st line R.	
			2 guns S. HEUDECOURT. Six guns of 218th M.G. Coy also occupied positions. These guns were with the No.4 Section 2nd LT WINE. R. N. of HEUDECOURT.	
		4.30 P.M	Command of O.C. Coy. The above relief was complete by 5.30 P.M.	
			O.C. Coy inspected the guns in their new positions.	J.B.
2nd		8 am	An enemy aeroplane fired on by A.A. from LIERAMONT was seen to fall in the area of Bn on our right.	
		9.15am	O.C. Coy visit Bde H.Q. returning at 1.30 P.M.	
		10.45 P.M	X VIth Corps M.G. officer visit Coy H.Q.	1 Officer in Trenches. J.B.
		3 P.M.	O.C. Coy went a tour of inspection returning at 6 P.M.	
3rd		9.15am	G.O.C. Coy reconnoitres with a view to placing guns in new positions concerning returning at 4.30 P.M.	
		1 P.M.	Lieutenant in cooperation with O.C.S. Bn visited Coy H.Q. where he took up his quarters.	
		5.30 P.M	X VIth Corps M.G. officer visited Bde H.Q.	
			O.C. Coy visits Bde H.Q.	
			LT FL BROOKS joins for duty from GRANTHAM. 60.O.R. joined.	J.B.
4		5.30 am	No.1 Section relieved No.3 Section at BUYENCOURT. No.3 Section then took up positions on the R4 between HEUDECOURT & PEIZIERE. 2 guns No.2 Section were moved into the line of Resistance 500 N.E. of SOREL LE GRAND.	
		9 am	O.C. Coy went a tour of inspection of the guns returning to Coy H.Q. at 2.30 P.M. after which he visited Bde H.Q.	
		3 P.M.	X VIth Corps M.G. officer Visits his Coy at Coy H.Q.	

2449 Wt. W14957/M90 750,000 1/16 J.B.C. & A. Forms/C.2118/12.

Army Form C. 2118.

WAR DIARY
or
INTELLIGENCE SUMMARY

(Erase heading not required.)

Instructions regarding War Diaries and Intelligence Summaries are contained in F.S. Regs., Part II. and the Staff Manual respectively. Title Pages will be prepared in manuscript.

Place	Date	Hour	Summary of Events and Information	Remarks and references to Appendices
LIERAMONT.	APRIL 4th	4.30 P.M.	O.C. Coy visited from Q No 3 Section. This section was prepared to cooperate with 25th Inf. Bn. in their attack on the ground W. of GOUZEAUCOURT. Heavy shelling in RAILTON & of GUYENCOURT.	J.W.B.
	5th	6.15 P.M. – 10 P.M.	During the morning O.C. Coy visited the guns. No 3 Section moved from RAILTON to position 100 x E. of "COPSE 2" & 300' S.E. of that place. No 4 Section moved 2 guns from position S.W. of HEUDICOURT to position S.E. of REVELON. During the night No 3 Section carried out fire on GAUCHE WOOD & GOUZEAUCOURT.	J.W.B.
		3 P.M.		
		8 P.M.	1 O.R. to hosp.	
HEUDICOURT.	6th	9.30 a.m.	Coy H.Q. moved to HEUDICOURT. This move was completed by 12 NOON. The following moves also took place:— No 1 Section relieved No 2 Section. No 2 Section under Lt BROOKS proceeded to HEUDICOURT. — 25-A- R.O. Coy now occupied & positions in the Reserve Line. — 2 guns Q 21.8.– M.G. Coy remained at LIERAMONT under Lt SEDDON.	J.W.B.
	7th	7 a.m.	No 2 Section under Lt BROOKS occupied 2 positions S.E. of Lisetem of FINS — GOUZEAUCOURT & HEUDICOURT — BRICAMP Rd. — 2 guns were placed in position 1000 x N.N. of REVELON on sunken road. These positions had been previously sited by O.C. Coy.	
		9.30 a.m.	O.C. Coy visited the guns. 1 O.R. from hosp. 2 O.R. to hosp.	
	8th	1 P.M.	Six guns of 219 R. D.O. Coy were withdrawn into reserve at HEUDICOURT. Of these, 2 guns were employed in A.A. work. During the afternoon D.C. Coy visited the guns in the Line. Coy E. Prinate at Coy H.Q. Conducted by Rev. A.D. MILLEN. Lt SEDDON took over the Command of No 2 Section from Lt BROOKS. 2 O.R. from hosp.	J.W.B.
		2.15 P.M.		
		6 P.M.		
	9th	10.30 a.m.	O.C. Coy visited the guns. O.C. Coy visited Bde H.Q. No 3 Section relieved No 1 Section at wiring gun position. This relief was complete by 4.30 P.M. 2nd commenced on	J.W.B.
		2.15 P.M.		

2449 Wt. W14957/M90 750,000 1/16 J.B.C. & A. Forms/C.2118/12.

WAR DIARY or INTELLIGENCE SUMMARY

Army Form C. 2118.

Place	Date	Hour	Summary of Events and Information	Remarks and references to Appendices
HEUDICOURT	APRIL 10th	11.15 am	O.C. Coy visited Bn. H.Q.	J.H.S.
		2.15 pm	O.C. Coy visited B.H.Q. where he conferred with C.O.	
		4 pm	218th M.G.Coy relieved No 2 Section. Relief complete at 4 pm.	B.O.157.
"	11th		Natural for moving wire carried to the Gun positions.	
		12 N.	O.C. Coy reconnoitred positions in the Coys of the Bn. Front. The Bn. are "side-slipping" roughly 200 x westwards, for the purpose of shortening to be carried out the following day. In conformity with this movement No 3 Section, on the right, No 1 Section at 2 pm & 210th T.B. Coy took up new position on the left at 7 pm. between QUEENS CROSS & FINS — GOUZEAUCOURT Rd. No 3 Section were withdrawn to Coy H.Q. This movement was complete by 12 midnight.	Offrs. Joined B.O.158.
"	12th	9.30 am	2nd Lt. MEESON joined for T.O. from GRANTHAM. O.C. Coy visited Bgde H.Q.	J.H.S.
		4 pm	No 2 Section relieved No 1 Section, whose Offr's Gun were placed at disposal of O.C. 1/5 Queens. No 2 Section moved from Coy H.Q. Indications took up position on Hill "135".	
		4.45 pm	REVELON — GOUZEAUCOURT Rd. where Guns Could be brought to bear on GOUZEAUCOURT. No 3 Section was at disposal of O.C. 2.E. LAN. R.	B.O.158.
		7 pm	Loco Gun 2-tin & 2/Lt. Inf. B.H.Q. carried out an attack with 3/Yuhen king GOUZEAUCOURT & line BAUCHE WOOD, MEUNIER HOUSE respectively. All objectives were taken.	
		2 am	2 GR. Finn Cards.	
"	13th	3 am	2/Lt. No 2 Section moved to position S.W. of GOUZEAUCOURT.	J.H.S.
		2 N.	O.C. Coy visited B.H.Q. Mr. Bicharter wounded. The following movements took place. 2 pm No 3 Section relieved 2 pm 237 T.B. Coy E. of QUENTIN MILL - This relief was complete by 9 pm. No 1 Section relieved 2 pm were relieved by 212 T.B. Coy returned to HEUDICOURT. No 2 Section relieved 4 pm 218th T.B. Coy — GOUZEAUCOURT Rd. 2 guns No 3 Section returned to Coy H.Q.	B.O.159.

S & F INS — GOUZEAUCOURT Rd.

2449 Wt. W14937/M90 750,000 1/16 J.B.C. & A. Forms/C.2118/12.

Army Form C. 2118.

WAR DIARY
or
INTELLIGENCE SUMMARY
(Erase heading not required.)

Instructions regarding War Diaries and Intelligence Summaries are contained in F. S. Regs., Part II. and the Staff Manual respectively. Title Pages will be prepared in manuscript.

Place	Date	Hour	Summary of Events and Information	Remarks and references to Appendices
HEUDICOURT	APRIL 14th	1 a.m.	Three ships were complete by 1 a.m. on the 14th inst.	J.B.
		11 a.m.	O.C. C07 finished at a Court-martial held at H.Q. 18 Wnc. R.	
		1 P.M.	O.C. C07 visited B.M.H.Q.	J.B.
		11 a.m.	No 1 Section & 2 guns 218th M.G. Co. moved to positions N & NE of GOUZEAUCOURT on sunken road leading to TRESCAULT & GONNELIEU respectively.	
"	15th	10 a.m.	O.C. C07 M.G. 18 guns returning at 2 P.M.	J.B.
		12 N.	Between 12 N & 4 P.M. 2000 R. first few rounds to fire in GONNELIEU from QUENTIN MILL. The C07 was visited by 25th M.G. Co. in the line returning to billets on the PERONNE Rd.	B.O. 162.
			S of NURLU. This relief was complete by 1 a.m. 4 guns of the C07 were detailed for A.A. duty as follows 2 guns No 2 station at MOISLAINS.	
			2 guns No 3 station LIERAMONT.	
			2 guns No 2 station and to XV.th Corps H.Q. know HAUT ALLAINES & were relieved by a	J.B.
NURLU	16th	9.30 a.m.	3 Sections of No 4 station.	
			Paris Shering. 12.30 P.M. An Officers Conference took place — Officers were informed	B.O. 163.
		11.30 a.m.	of points to be taken up in the event of attack.	
		2 P.M.	Pack Shering & Gun Mus-at.	
		6.30 A.M.	2 Teams No 2 Station returned to Co 7. H.Q. from XV.th Corps H.Q. Substation no 4 station remaining at MOISLAINS under 2M SEDDON.	
"	17th		The Morning Changes in Dispositions 2 A.A. guns took effect. 1 gun No 1 Station SOREL 1 gun No 4 Station AZIECOURT. 2 guns from LIERAMONT with Teams. 1 gun No 4 Station moved at NURLU. 2 guns No 3 Station remained at NURLU.	

WAR DIARY or INTELLIGENCE SUMMARY

Army Form C. 2118.

(Erase heading not required.)

Instructions regarding War Diaries and Intelligence Summaries are contained in F. S. Regs., Part II. and the Staff Manual respectively. Title Pages will be prepared in manuscript.

Place	Date	Hour	Summary of Events and Information	Remarks and references to Appendices
NURLU	APRIL 17th 1917	6.P.M.	No 3 Section moved off to occupy positions in the "BROWN LINE". The two left guns were placed in position by LT BROOKS & the two right guns by 2/LT PLUE. Ammunition in charge of the position. This movement being completed by 11.P.M. 2T NEALE became A/O.C. Co.7 & LT BEECHMAN A/2 i/c command.	J.B.
	17th	N.K.	O.C. Co.7 accompanied by LT HIGHAM visited the guns in the "BROWN LINE" returning to Co.7 H.Q. at 6.P.M.	J.B.
	18th.	2.30P.M.	The Co.7 moved to billets in LIERAMONT.	
LIERAMONT	19th.	7am	A.A. team with Drum from AIZECOURT-LE-BAS. AA. team No 4 Section stationed at GUYENCOURT.	
		2 P.M.	O.C. No 1 Section & O.C. No 4 Section reconnoitred the Tortille-stick train (between line of) Resistance & the BROWN LINE.	J.B.
		2.30 P.M.	Co.7 was found out at LIERAMONT. The remainder on AA. Duty & at Transport were sent out in the following day.	
		3.30 P.M.	O.C. Co.7 visited AA. gun at GUYENCOURT. 1 OR. 6 hop.	
	20th.	7 am	Breakfasts. 9 am Co.7 paraded for G.O.C. 9th Division's inspection. This was his Swg. NURLU at 10.30 am.	
		2 P.M	O.C. Co.7 reconnoitred his 9 wdrance returning at 7 p.m.	
		2.30 A.M.	No 3 Section relieved No 3 Section in the BROWN LINE returning to billets at 8 P.M. No 2 Section relieved No 3 pumby. 10 R pumby. 4 OR. Joined.	J.B.

2449 Wt. W14957/M90 750,000 1/16 J.B.C. & A. Forms/C.2118/12.

WAR DIARY or INTELLIGENCE SUMMARY

Army Form C. 2118.

(Erase heading not required.)

Place	Date	Hour	Summary of Events and Information	Remarks and references to Appendices
LIERAMONT	APRIL 21st	9 am	Breakfast. 9 am Trinity Room. 9.30 – 10.30 Section Parade.	J/B
		10.30 am	O.C. Co. visited B'de H.Q. after which he marched from No 2 Section.	
		11.45"	Coy. Para eyes for R.A.R.S. at MOISLAINS allotted from 2 P.M – 3 P.M.	J/B
		2.15 PM	LT BEECHMAN reconnoitred position held by right B.de. (2.30) returning at 6 P.M. There were baths for the remainder of Co.	
"	22nd	9 am	Breakfast. 9.15 am Trinity Room. 10 am Coy Parade.	
			Coy on the firing range. 2/Lt SULLY & 2/Lt PITT reconnoitred area occupied by right B.de returning at 7 P.M.	
		1 P.M.	O.C. Coy accompanied by 2/Lt H.Q. attended by A/Lt in command	J/B
		6.30 PM	O.C.'s conference at B'de H.Q. visited at MOISLAINS by 2/Lt M.G. Coy.	
			Subsection of No 4 section released by SOREL released by 2 & 4 M.G. Coy.	
"	23rd	9.30 am	A.A. gun at NURLU was relieved by 2/Lt T & Coy. H.A. gun at LIERAMONT.	B.O. 166.
		3 PM	A.A. gun at GUYENCOURT was Westbourne, also A.A. gun at LIERAMONT.	
			The Co. stations No. 2 & 3 M.G. Coy in the line. Coy H.Q. was at CHAPEL CROSSING.	
			No. 2 Section – No. 3 Section occupied positions in the new BLUE (in SUPPORT) LINE.	J/B
CHAPEL CROSSING			No 1 Section & No 4 Section occupied positions in the GREEN LINE (in Front line + lines of Resistance).	
	24th	12.30 am	This night was spent by 1/2 12.30 am.	
		1.45 am	O.C. Coy returned after visiting guns, at 1.45 am.	
		9.30 am	O.C. Coy visited the gun returning at 11.30 am. Coy Transport arrived from MOISLAINS to NURLU.	
		8 P.M.	No 1 Section moved to advanced position 600 X N.W. HONNECOURT WOOD	
		8.15 PM	2 guns visited by O.C. Coy who returned at 11.30 am.	
"	25-	10 am	O.C. Coy visited guns in the line.	J/B
		11 am	2 guns N.E. of GAUCHE WOOD was blown in. This gun + 2 R.	
			an emplacement occupied by No 2 Section E. of GAUCHE WOOD was blown in.	
			The German being heavy. The gun was not put out of action.	
		4 P.M.	O.C. Coy visited B'de H.Q. & afterwards O.C. 2 NNkR.	
		6.30 AM	O.C. Coy visited No 1 gun in the line + was put in position to cover 1 gun (No 1 Section) forward to cover an advance by 2 NORTH'R towards HONNECOURT.	

Army Form C. 2118.

WAR DIARY
or
INTELLIGENCE SUMMARY
(Erase heading not required.)

Instructions regarding War Diaries and Intelligence Summaries are contained in F. S. Regs., Part II. and the Staff Manual respectively. Title Pages will be prepared in manuscript.

Place	Date	Hour	Summary of Events and Information	Remarks and references to Appendices
CHAPEL CROSSING	APRIL 26th		Communication was established with 126th M.G. Coy on our right which a view to cooperation. 4 guns 218th M.G. Coy relieved No 3 Section who went into reserve at VILLERS GUISLAINS. This relief was completed at 6 P.M. O.C. Coy took up his position at VILLERS GUISLAINS. 2 O.R. wounded at hrq. 1 O.R. to hrq.	7/B.
VILLERS GUISLAINS.	27th	6.30 AM	Rear Coy H.Q. was moved into advanced Coy Hq at VILLERS GUISLAINS. Fire was carried out on enemy between GONNELIEU & BANTEUX. An intermittent artillery duel petters. No 2 Section relieved No 4 Section in the right & No 3 Section relieved No 1 Section on the left. The relief came back into reserve in Coy H.Q. 1 gun of No 4 Section was placed in support line on the right 1000 x S.W. of HONNECOURT. 2 O.R. from hospital.	7/B.
"	28th		Rear Coy was issued with steel waistcoats. Enemy 2.6.K. Fire was kept on enemy communication W. of BANTEUX. 1 O.R. to hrq. 1 O.R. from hrq.	7/B.
"	29th		During friendly fire weather there were no great activity which the enemy appeared to have experienced. 4 Enemy planes manoeuvred over VILLERS GUISLAINS dropping bombs in TARGELLE RAVINE and HONNECOURT WOOD & HUNNECOURT between 9 P.M. & 11 P.M. No serious damage was caused. 1 O.R. wounded. 1 O.R. from hrq.	7/B.
"	30th	6.30 PM 9 PM	Enemy shelled 4 guns of No 4 Section & No 2 Section in TARGELLE RAVINE firing the morning. O.C. Coy visited the forward sites & picked a position in the support line W. of HONNECOURT WOOD. Decision for new emmission was no serious difference in the BANTEUX POSITION	7/B.

Albert Ind
O.C. 24 M.G.Y.

War Diary
of the
24th Machine Gun Company.
for the
month of May 1917 by
Major E.E.C.Lewis.

WAR DIARY
or
INTELLIGENCE SUMMARY

(Erase heading not required.)

Army Form C., 2118.

Place	Date	Hour	Summary of Events and Information	Remarks and references to Appendices
VILLERS GUISLAIN	May 1st	10.15 A.M.	There was heavy shelling in the area occupied by the Brigade all day to West & far of Champion. Two killed & 2 O.R. wounded. No 3 subin in "D" gun position on VILLERS GUISLAIN — HONNECOURT Rd. Pte Rattyffe No 8 section wounded while in Reserve at Coy H.Q. 9 emplacements No 4 section in GREEN LINE in TARRELLE RAVINE were blown in. An interbattalion relief took place – No 1 section relieved No 3 section in left subsector of Brigade front – No 4 section relieved No 2 in right subsector.	M.
			No 3 section occupied the green line. No. 2. section being in Reserve. Relief complete. Indirect fire was carried out on the southern defences of LA VACQUERIE during the night.	
	2nd	1.00 P.M. 3 A.M. to 5 A.M. 8 P.M.	Enemy artillery very active and bombs dropped from aeroplanes on the village. O.C. Coy returned from leave. O.C. Coy visited guns in GREEN LINE. D.C. (O) visited forward guns accompanied by 2nd in Command. Indirect fire was carried out on enemy defences S. of BANTEUX. Anti aircraft gun manned by No 2 section in village.	M.
	3rd	9-10 A.M. 9 P.M.	Aerial activity over village. Enemy machines were fired on from our A.A. gun in village and driven back to their lines. O.C. Company selected barrage positions for gun N.E. of the village for operations on May 5th inst.	M/s

Army Form C. 2118.

WAR DIARY
or
INTELLIGENCE SUMMARY

(Erase heading not required.)

Instructions regarding War Diaries and Intelligence Summaries are contained in F. S. Regs., Part II. and the Staff Manual respectively. Title Pages will be prepared in manuscript.

Place	Date	Hour	Summary of Events and Information	Remarks and references to Appendices
VILLERS GUISLAIN	May 3rd (cont.)		The gun positions in the GREEN LINE were also altered with a view to better fields of fire being obtained. No 1 section, 1 gun No 4 section, 1 gun No 3 section carried out indirect fire on defences S. of BANTEUX, & on HONNECOURT WOOD from 11.30 P.M. and intermittently throughout the night. No 1 section travel gun engaged enemy battle gun in HONNECOURT WOOD with direct fire at 11 P.M. This gun was silenced. Rifle grenades were fired on advanced gun of No 4 section in Right Sub sector at 10 P.M.	M.
	4th		Three enemy aeroplanes passed over northern end of VILLERS GUISLAIN at 5.20 P.M. They attacked and destroyed a British observation balloon. Indirect fire was carried out by 3 guns No 1 section and 1 gun No 2 section on water R.29 c 20.42; M.G. at × nearby R 28 d. 05.30. M.G. at R 29 c.40.52; R 29 C. 4.5.	M.

Army Form C. 2118.

WAR DIARY
or
INTELLIGENCE SUMMARY
(Erase heading not required.)

Instructions regarding War Diaries and Intelligence Summaries are contained in F. S. Regs., Part II. and the Staff Manual respectively. Title Pages will be prepared in manuscript.

Place	Date	Hour	Summary of Events and Information	Remarks and references to Appendices
VILLERS GUISLAIN (contd)	May 4th		Ammunition, water and belt boxes were carried up to barrage positions N. of village. Lieut T.J. Beecham proceeded on leave to Paris. Extract from XI Corps Intelligence summary 5th May 1917. "Enemy M.G. at X 11.c.2.1. has been persistently active; A M.G. at X 11.b.1.2. was silenced by the fire of our M.G.'s.	J.M.
	May 5th	1 P.M.	Enemy aerial activity was less than usual. Nos 2 & 3 sections in positions about 300x N.E. end of village. carried out a barrage on enemy defences in R 29 c & D. and R 35 a. 50,000 rounds were fired. Enemy retaliation was slight. This barrage was in conjunction with a raid by 2/Devons & 2/Middlesex 13°° J.b Bde to SONNET FARM to secure identification and destroy enemy morale. Only 2 O.R. reached SONNET FARM and they withdrew on finding it strongly held. A white very light handing into 4 was observed 9.40 A.M. in R 28. No apparent action followed.	J.M.

WAR DIARY
or
INTELLIGENCE SUMMARY

(Erase heading not required.)

Army Form C. 2118.

Place	Date	Hour	Summary of Events and Information	Remarks and references to Appendices
VILLERS GUISLAIN	May 6th	5.5 P.M.	Enemy aeroplane passed over village and was fired on by our A.A. gun. Enemy observation balloon was seen to fall in flames near LATEAU	M.
		6.15 P.M.	WOOD.	
		7 P.M.	Seven hostile machines passed over village. They attacked one of our aeroplanes and compelled it to descend near VENDHUILE.	
		12 Midnight	A.A. gun of No. 1 Section fired from X 5 c 5.0. at farm X 11 + 19. which were heard by tgt. It firing and by several officers and men in the front line. 1 O.R. from hospital.	
	7th	9.5 A.M.	A.A. gun in VILLERS GUISLAIN fired 250 rounds at hostile machine range 900 ft. Aeroplane was seen to fall behind enemy lines in direction of BANTOUZELLE. An later section relief took place. No. 3 section relieved No. 1 in left subsection, brigade front. No. 2 section relieved No 4 section in right subsection of brigade front. No 4 section came back into reserve in village. No 1 Section occupied GREEN LINE. LIEUT. F. L. BROOKS to hospital.	M.

Army Form C. 2118.

WAR DIARY
or
INTELLIGENCE SUMMARY
(Erase heading not required.)

Instructions regarding War Diaries and Intelligence Summaries are contained in F. S. Regs., Part II. and the Staff Manual respectively. Title Pages will be prepared in manuscript.

Place	Date	Hour	Summary of Events and Information	Remarks and references to Appendices
VILLERS GUISLAINS	MAY 8th	1.30 a.m. 6 p.m.	Four yellow flying lights were seen to the right of HONNECOURT. Wet weather prevailed. O.C. (O.C.) visits front.	7ths.
" LIERAMONT	9th		Fine weather. Relief by 23rd M.G. Co. took place. The Co. proceeded into billets at LIERAMONT with the exception of No 4 Section who occupied A.A. positions in HEUDICOURT (2 guns) LIERAMONT (1 gun) SOREL-LE-GRAND 1 gun. This relief was complete by midnight.	7ths.
"	10th	1 p.m. 4 p.m.	Morning spent cleaning kit, equipment etc. The Co. was present. 1 O.R. down to O.K.	7ths.
"	11th	9.30 am 10.30am 12.30pm 1 p.m. 1 p.m.	The Co. was inspected by G.O.C. 2 i/c of Bn. who ran the "MILL" LIERAMONT. Horse Ride, Physical Training + Drill under Coys animals. Baths given. Lectures to O.C. in use afternoon at MOISLAINS. The Co. moves to billets in MOISLAINS leaving LIERAMONT at 1 p.m. An advance following party proceeds under 2nd Lt W. SEDDON. MOISLAINS was reached at 3.30 pm. A.A. positions at LIERAMONT were taken by 23rd M.G. Co. Lt W. Def. McAdam 2-3 M.G. Co. A.A. positions at HEUDICOURT and SOREL-LE-GRAND by 123rd M.G. Co. 2nd in Coy. Roum.	7ths. B.O. 175.
MOISLAINS	12th	4 p.m.	2 A.A. positions were manned near C.H.Q. (A) Transport moved from NURLU to MOISLAINS. Transport Lines near MOISLAINE CHURCH.	7ths.
	13th	9.30 am 10.30am	8 Trifferds sent to 10th X V Corps for purpose of reboaking + overhauling. Inspection Parade including kit inspection. 1 O.R. from hosp.	7ths.
	14th	9.30 am	1 O.R. to hosp. Guns No 1 + No 2 inspected. Had the presence of instructors accompanied of O.C. Ammunition Parade re: Breakfast 7.30 am. P.T. 8.30 - 9 am. Squad Drill 9.15 - 9.45. Cleaning of guns kit 10.15-12am. Inspection of all guns kit by O.C. Co. 2.30 - 5.30 pm. Webbing, Packs, 1 officers + 30 O.R. returns to Staff Captain for work in Bn. H.Q. 1 O.R. from hosp.	7ths.

Army Form C. 2118.

WAR DIARY
or
INTELLIGENCE SUMMARY.
(Erase heading not required.)

Instructions regarding War Diaries and Intelligence Summaries are contained in F. S. Regs., Part II. and the Staff Manual respectively. Title pages will be prepared in manuscript.

Place	Date	Hour	Summary of Events and Information	Remarks and references to Appendices
HOULAINS	MAY 1918		Programme of work as above. — PT 8.30 – 9 am. Supers + rifle drill 9.15 – 10.30 am. Bathing of Platoon 10 – 12 noon.	T/R.
		PT 12 NOON – 12.15 Preparation. 2 – 3pm.	
		3.pm	As working party, consisting of 1 officer + 60 O.R. reported to Staff Capt. & not in use. P.R. M.O.	T/R.
		6.45pm	At A.V. Hall. Relieved & return to Officers + N.C.O.'s. Retired Burning + Saluting.	
	16th		Programme of Training. P.T. 8.15 – 9.05. Squad + rifle drill 9 – 9.30am. Sem – drill 10 – 11 am. Bayonet Fighting by Bn'd 10-12 noon. P.T. 12 – 12.30 Physical Training. L of Becher Shrine "Gas".	T/R.
	17th		Programme of Training included P.T. 8.15 – 8.45 Squad + rifle drill 9 – 10 am. Range 10 – 12 noon. P.T. 12 – 12.30. Lecture on all officers + e.Q.M. + station by G. O.C. Bn to B Coy 5pm. Officers + N.C.O's prior to visit to the H.of B. Rehearsal bataille, including G.O.C. 2nd out of bg. MG, Lewis + officers + M.O. 8 P.T. 7pm - & Staff the Suffering.	M.R.
	18		Programme of work as before: — P.T. 8.15 – 8.05 am. Squad + rifle drill 9 – 10am and bomblery of Grenades 10 – 10.45am. Bombs & attack of grenades + machine in action 1 – 1.30 am. At 11 noon G.O.C. & H.Q. Corps. Will inspect H troops at MILLS WOOD near HORLU No 1. Lecture reported at H.Q. at 2 pm with R.I.M.V. Bn C. Capt Tomlinson was present as M.M. and D. C. M. 2pm. – 3pm. L.O.R. from hosp.	T/R.
	19		Programme of work as before: — 7.30 Breakfast. 8.15 – 9 am. Parade 9 – 9.45 Revolut. 10 – 12 noon Range.	T/R.
			PT. 12 – 12.30. PT. 2 – 3pm. Lewis gun. W/M Relieved Battalion.	
	20	P.m.	Church Parade for N.C.O.s at 9.45 – for C.of E. at 9.30am.	T/R.
		6pm.	Inspection of Fire Station by Capt. Sec. C O's on Lewis art.	
	21		Programme of Training included: — 9am. Physical training 9 – 9.30 drill with rifles 9.30 – 12.30 occupation of position in battle trenches. Relief of working Canada attacks. Lecture by St. Lt. Comp. D.O.O. – 7pm O.C. Co's, agreed officers & N.C.O's in period arriving from above.	T/R.
	2pm		LOTR from hosp. C.S.M. Wilson & Mullett him to U.K.	

(A7592). Wt. W12859/M1293. 75,000. 1/17. D. D. & L., Ltd. Forms/C.2118/14.

Army Form C. 2118.

WAR DIARY
or
INTELLIGENCE SUMMARY.
(Erase heading not required.)

Instructions regarding War Diaries and Intelligence Summaries are contained in F. S. Regs., Part II. and the Staff Manual respectively. Title pages will be prepared in manuscript.

Place	Date	Hour	Summary of Events and Information	Remarks and references to Appendices
FIGEONS	MAY 22		Wet weather. Programme of training restricted to P.T. — Rifle PT. 9 — 12 noon. Backing up E.S. after Dejeun. & continue was inspected by so far Divisional. All Ranks were inspected. Afternoon free owing to rain. 7 pm. Lecture by Lt. SEcretion. Bombing.	Offrs.
	23	3 am.	G.O.C. No 5 Coy. Capt. Edmunds & detm. to Mr. Sman NCOs & Offrs. MT. A/C.COs Grimm & 6 orderlies by 6t. attend riot duties. 10 am. Ceremonial. Presentation of Training Activities P.T. — P.T.&R.C.O. 9 am — 9.30 am Drill & Musketry 9.30 — 11.30 Rug. 2 pm — 4 pm Field drill. Army-musing manoeuvres. Bat Orders. 130 Lecture extended order drill for officers & N.C.O.s 7 pm to 8 pm	W6. 1Offrs joined.
	24		1 Offr & 11 batt Griffiths joined from CLIPSTONE. Programme of work as above. P.T. 7.15 — 8.45 — Drill & Musketry 9 — 9.20. Bat. Army & musketry of R.O. position for shoulder. R.C. Recruits G. Bo — 12.30pm Ranges 2 pm 6 pm — 7 pm Seu No 2 Lecture (Bayonette). 7 pm Lecture to Officers & N.C.Os by Col Col — No 3 Lecture was attended by 1st SHEA. F. & Officer in Absequrt as shoot in the morning. 10am bath for UK	W6.
	25		Programme of Training inclusive — P.15 — 2.45pm. 9 — 9.30 Musketry. 9.30 — 12.30 Rel. firing 2 — 3 pm. Musketry 3 pm — 4 pm Rest firing. No 2 Lecture Lt Mehnen an checked & 2 E. Laws A. for training area in VILLE WOOD in the morning. No 1 Lecture was finished 4tended to 1 Office. F. in galley our MPHILAINS. 6 pm hem — Rifle Grenades No 3 Lecture.	W6.
	26		Programme of work inclusive P.T. 8 am — 9.4.5. Drill & Musketry 9 — 9.30 am. Squad & Army Drill 9.30 — 10 am. Rifle — 30 mins, 10 — 12 — 30 Range field firing 2 — 2.30 Entrenched Drill 2.30 — 4 pm Bed-filling by sections & Ptching of whirl belts. 6 pm. Sec. Rifle Grenades. No 2 Lecture All Handles were returned to Reference Me 2 & 4 friends at Camp 21 on Route are to Bat. Transport Officer.	W6.

(A7092). Wt. W1289/M1293. 750,000. 1/17. D. D. & L., Ltd. Forms/Cart8/14.

Army Form C. 2118

WAR DIARY
or
INTELLIGENCE SUMMARY.
(Erase heading not required.)

Instructions regarding War Diaries and Intelligence Summaries are contained in F. S. Regs., Part II. and the Staff Manual respectively. Title pages will be prepared in manuscript.

Place	Date	Hour	Summary of Events and Information	Remarks and references to Appendices
MORLANCOURT	MAY 27		M.C. Lecture 11 am. C.O.'s Lecture 11.30 am – at HQ/Coys.	F/B.
	28		Programme of Work includes PT 8.15 – 8.45. Musketry 9 am – 9.30 am. Range 9.30 to 12.30 pm. Baths, filling & packing of Limbers 2 – 4 pm.	F/B.
	29		The 24th Inf Bn commenced a march to CORBIE to entrain. The 24th M.G. Coy paraded to Band, in SUZANNE. Time table as under. – Reveille 4.30 am, Parade 6.30 am, 2nd Pln.	F/B. B.O. 176.
CAMP AT SUZANNE			paraded in advance to fill up. ROUTE :– HAUTALLAINES (Starting Point) – CLERY-MARICOURT – SUZANNE. The Coy arrived in camp at 11.30 am. B.O.C. 8th Divn reviewed the Column on the march S of HAUTALLAINES. Tpn M arrived 12 noon.	
	30		Parade. Lewis Parties 9.30 am. Reveille at 4 pm – Feb 11.15 – 12.15. Coy Parade 2 – 3 pm.	F/B.
	31		Rest of night kept free. The 24th M.G. Coy moved into billet in SAILLY LAURETTE. Reveille 5 am. Coy paraded at 7.10 am. Pte 281 W. SEDDON (No.)	F/B. B.O. 177.
			in advance to fill up. The Transport paraded in two Echelons – "A" fighting Limbers + H.Qrs. Limber, Echelon B. the remainder of the Transport. Starting point junction of	
SAILLY LAURETTE			BRAY-SUZANNE "Dust Road" + BRAY SUZANNE "Pavé Road." 7.47 am. ROUTE BRAY, BRAY-CORBIE ROAD – SAILLY LAURETTE. The Coy's Cookers parked on the march to prepare	
			dinner at the rail crossing. SAILLY LAURETTE was no nearer to reach in the first area owing to pack horses.	

J.S.C. Venour – Major
Cmdg. 24th M.Gun Coy.

War Diary
of the
27th Machine Gun Company.
for the month of
June 1917
by.
Captain A. M. Pratt.

WAR DIARY / INTELLIGENCE SUMMARY

Army Form C. 2118.

Place	Date	Hour	Summary of Events and Information	Remarks and references to Appendices
SAILLY LAURETTE	JUNE 1	6 am	The C.O. moved from SAILLY-LAURETTE to CORBIE. 2/Lt SEDDON proceeded to reconnoitre draining field.	B.O. 177
			Meanwhile Coy paraded for m The Transport under Lieut EDELSTEN in "A" and "B" echelons proceeded to	
CORBIE		11.30am	CORBIE via SAILLY-LAURETTE — (Packing point) — SAILLY-LE-SEC —	B.O. 177
			VAUX-S-SOMME — CORBIE (H.Q.)	
		2.30PM	Lt 2/Lt 78 OR reported to the A.P.M. of the Place Trêves (N.B.S. platoon)	
			relieved by No.3 platoon at 10.15 pm, and later for the week, 2/pms by No.18 M.G.Coy	
	2	10 am	were under the orders of the 24th M.G. Coy for this duty.	
		1 pm	A.class Lecture by Capt BLANKERS to 2 pm. & Reference — but	
			Capt transport of Coy transport by Q.O. Coys	
		5.30 pm	Inspected of Coy transport of CORBIE	
			The H.Q & 2 Coys entrained at CORBIE with orders to move into the HAZEBROUCK area	
		8 pm	Transport moved to CORPS PARK Refilling Point preliminary at CORBIE STN at 8 pm (No.14 Train)	B.O. 179
	3	9.30 am	Moving at 8.12 a.m. The C.O. arrived in Auto. ROUTE via ABBEVILLE — CALAIS —	MP
			ST OMER — HAZEBROUCK. Detraining took GODEWAERSVELDE (army at 8, from 3.50 pm)	
			Parade and filling party followed to billets, L/C to billets Flet., Lt HARRIS with a working	
			party. It is only No.3 platoon up to training. The Coy is engaging the H.Q.	
			& becomes at billet BIBLIOTHèque — Coy orders at MERRIS 1st H.Q. & 2nd M.Q.	
MERRIS	4	10 am	Mess also returned to MERRIS. Transport lines at EATSW.W of village	B.O. 180
		9.30 to 12.30	W officers v W officers in billets	
			S.O.R. to both	
			W S.O.R. to both — 2 June kit	
		2.30 pm	Heavy parade, handed of same kit. Instructions issued as to sight training trees — 5mm.	MP
			Major Seine asked to commence the C.O. proceeded via motor car to 4 MGTC GRANTHAM, ENGLAND	1 Offer
		5.15	2/Lt BEECHMAN was instructed to command. It then proceeded to/on Command	
			following [illegible] Major F.G. ADAMS to ENGLAND. Authority A/6864 G.H.Q. 2/6/18	
			Major F.G. ADAMS to ENGLAND.	

Army Form C. 2118.

WAR DIARY
or
INTELLIGENCE SUMMARY.

(Erase heading not required.)

Instructions regarding War Diaries and Intelligence Summaries are contained in F. S. Regs., Part II. and the Staff Manual respectively. Title pages will be prepared in manuscript.

Place	Date	Hour	Summary of Events and Information	Remarks and references to Appendices
MESSINES	JUNE 5	7.30 P.T. CAMP. 9.30 – 10.30am Gun point field. 10.30 – 11.30 Semaphore. 11.30 – 12.30 P.T. Papers 2-3 PM with papers 2-3 PM	MB
		1 PM	The parade turned over to the transport lines. The curb looked on the new Battle Line 3-5 PM.	
	6.		Oc 87 attending a conference at B.H.Q. 3 OR-TI/lot.	
		9.30 am	OC Companies by MILKY WAY (no RIFLEMEN permitted in the trenches) OR what was on G.H.Q. orders, and appeared to come in to return as the Battle of MESSINES actually lasting. 9.30 – 10.30 P.T. Semaphore. Talking by Divisional N.C.O. 10.30 – Bn. J.D. and V.T. 2 – 3 pm 6pm inspection of FCB 7 number by OC COY	B.O. 181
	7.	9am	P.T. Etc. C. 7 in by MO. Inspection. Could not trace Hutley. 9.30 – 10 A round to Alignment. 10.30 – 11.30 Lecture by MC CO. on Gathering of prisoners opposite. 1.30 – 12.30	MB.
			Notices sent out 11 – 3 PM. Guidance at BT. HQ followed by OC and MO and address communications. 2/Lt NELSON (CO370) RECEIVED BASE DEPOT under orders 1TR. tern Inf.	1.44 pm to report to OP 10.
	8.	7.30 am – 9am	P.T. 9.30 am G.O.C. 2nd Lt INF DIV inspected the COY turning parade 10 – 10.30. Musketry on hill. 10.30 – 11.30 hand of relieving ammunition. 1.30 – 12.30 Lecture by Lt A.V. SULLY Subject : Not 9 Dir in Bns Attn. 1-3 pm. OC Pratt – F.O. 1 CR 4 lot.	MB.
			17 DEANS joined from Base before an F.O.	
	9.	7.30 – 8am	P.T. 9.30 – 12.30 Ceremonial and Bill Point B.A. = A. Fenny ", Rev & Bayonet " and lecture by 2/Lt GRIFFITHS. 2.30 PM. OC COY inspected at Lew WAR	MB.

LT AM PRATT ATT ROYAL F. Command of the Coy. Joining from 28/17.6.COY

ALLMUMR XIX 1st Croft. A/8892 M. 26.5.17.

LT AM PRATT
1st Gweenw

WAR DIARY
or
INTELLIGENCE SUMMARY.
(Erase heading not required.)

Army Form C. 2118.

Place	Date	Hour	Summary of Events and Information	Remarks and references to Appendices
MERRIS	JUNE 10		Church Service for N.C.O's & men in C of E & R.C.'s at 10 a.m.	M/s
"	11		In-Sy'y Bn moved to CAESTRE arr. 24th M.G. Coy moved to SYLVESTER CAPEL on Main Road	B.O. 182
SYLVESTER CAPEL			CAESTRE - CAPEL Route via METEREN and CAESTRE. Two halts. Reveille 4.30 am. Breakfast 5 am. C'y moved off at 7.15 am. 2/Lt SEDDON proceeded in advance to billets. New billets reached 12 N.	M/s B.O.183
"	12		Th. 24 K.M.G. Coy moved to SCOTTISH CAMP in OUDERDOM - G. 23. a. 90.80 arriving 11:45	
			Camp at L. 30 d. 7. A bath was used in S.E. RENINGHELST at 11. 65 am Aug 3 PM. A route March to hear Divisional [?] (G. 30, 6, 14). The Coy moved off at 3 PM to the Camp (Route via EECKE)	
BELGIUM			LEDDESWAERVELDE - RENINGHELST - 1 OR from hosp.	
SCOTTISH CAMP	13		Parade 9-9.30 Man of Night firing tax 9.30-10 Lecture by 2/Lt C83 [?] for practice	M/s
		10.30 am	All Officers of the Bn [?] instructed & reported by G.O.C. II Corps on B.E. H.Q.	
		4.00	O.C. Coys & 2nd in command of 2/Lt SEDDON reconnoitres him & management was [?]	
			Io path no line from S.S. 4. 11.6.4. M.G. Coy's, positions & upper right entrance defined.	
			Normal. Returning from Rest for Funerals.	
	14	4 P.M.	O.C. Coys present in advance of site to reconnoitre & confirm the arrangements for [?]	M/s
		6 P.M.	Coys moved off from SCOTTISH CAMP with N. BEECHMAN. A halt was made at VLAMERTINGHE from 7.30 Pm. until 8.10 S.M. where a hasty dinner in consumed [?] D.O. H.Q. (2/Lt SEDDON) No 2 Section (Lt HIGHAM) Reach 116. M.G. Coy on its right N.G. MENIN Road 2/Lt GRIFFITHS post in charge of 2 forms a suffice [?]	B.O. 180 [?] 9.0.O.L. (thrice) Appendix B

Army Form C. 2118.

WAR DIARY
or
INTELLIGENCE SUMMARY.
(Erase heading not required.)

Instructions regarding War Diaries and Intelligence Summaries are contained in F.S. Regs., Part II. and the Staff Manual respectively. Title pages will be prepared in manuscript.

Place	Date	Hour	Summary of Events and Information	Remarks and references to Appendices
YPRES (LINE). HOOGE SECTOR	JUNE 14.		No. 3 Section 2/Lt Paul assumed 9.O. of H.Q. Coy. in replacement of 2/Lt Western wounded on 13th. Infantry Bomb YPRES Co. H.Q. Bogue in Canada R.N.N. Shoes away unacclimated from 15-6-17. OC. Coy. accompanied by O.C. 90 M.G. Coy. visited the front line in Hot Pries.	Coy. O.C.'s MB Appendix MB B
	15	4 a.m.	"M.G. Coy at BLUE GATE (party N°1) returned.	MB
		9 a.m.	1 gun (N° L Baker) relieved from gun 9.O.S. C.H. Right 7 Runaway Guns (party N° 1 return to MENIN ROAD relieved by 166 M.G. Coy. (3 N°1 Section & A.O.P. (Baker) gun relieved in section by 20 M.G. Coy. This being completed gun to gun ran mount) LIVERPL E reports from Halting place PIERCOURT	
	16	4 a.m.	O.C. Coy. and 2 off. in Armoured (LIVERPL E) Arrived on fore of infantry relief at gun returning at P.M.	MB
		12.30 p.m.	8 Aux M.G. 0. Visits Coy. H.Q.	
		3 p.m.	2nd in command visited the guns. The Heal accompanied by 2/Lt GRIFFITHS who relieved is now to remands. There were very telling of the attack on YPRES on Iron track open and	
	17		YPRES heavily Shelled 5.9 16.15 am - 3.30 p.m. wounding vicinity of Coy. H.Q. D.C. Coy. accompanied by 2/Lt JEDDON proceeds to ZOUAVE WOOD in van to sell 4 H.G. position	MB
		3 p.m.		
		4 p.m.	N° 3 Section proceeds to load in this a new order run to 2/Lt JEDDON who guides them this entrenched BARRAGE POSITIONS SE of HALFWAY HO 2/Lt JEDDON wounded also 1 Ptl. & SOR. 1 Officer SOR. so not wounded.	

WAR DIARY
or
INTELLIGENCE SUMMARY.

Army Form C. 2118.

Place	Date	Hour	Summary of Events and Information	Remarks and references to Appendices
YPRES TRENCHES	June 18		C.O. H.Q. and remnants of 9 HOATED GRANGE Shellholes during the morning. No 20 & 21 M.G. C.O. were relieved in the line by No 2/8th M.G. C.O. (Appendix 23 M.G.C.O.)	
HOOGE SECTOR			H.Q. No 2 section N.S. infantry taken voluntary line at LILLE GATE and relieved at	
		11.00 p.m.	Enemy's heavy shelling of the approaches to YPRES. No relief 1/2 C.O. proceeded on the march from YPRES to No 3 Section Q. No. 2 Section, & C. each new Camp HALIFAX CAMP	
		1.30 a.m. 19/6	1/2 C.O. movement of H.Q. to no relief current road.	B.O.
40 HALIFAX CAMP V.19			KRUISSTRAAT - BELGIAN CHATEAU - X ROADS DEN GRENEN	186.-
JAGER - HALIFAX CAMP.				
		Morning	Blessant Parade. Bath at HALIFAX CAMP for the W.A.M.C.	
HALIFAX CAMP IN VLAMERTINGHE	19th		The remainder of the camp was less than 3 less than shelling continuance intermittently especially on upper thoroughfare when Coy. were despatched HALIFAX CAMP -	
	20th		A column of 7 gap parading were observed. Route curtailed For a stretching infantry as to, also taught approximately right quarters yes. New afternoon by enemy, interns. German line, Zero jolts, was despatched by C.O. & received by C.O's respective.	
			Morreton at Frommy. O.C.C inspection B.W.S, Refreshm 6a.m — 7.45 a.m Morreton 6 a.m. Drill. 7 – 7.30 a.m Repairs Bath. Inspection knots of learning	M.S.

WAR DIARY
or
INTELLIGENCE SUMMARY.
(Erase heading not required.)

Army Form C. 2118.

Place	Date	Hour	Summary of Events and Information	Remarks and references to Appendices
HALIFAX CAMP	JUNE 20	9 am	Lecture by O.C. Coy to Officers N.C.Os and O.R. From previous Subject 2 ENEMY LINES. Remainder of Coy helped in construction of BARRAGE trenches. H & N section parties in Lecture on Elementary 12 – 12.30 TO E.T. 2 – 2.45 Musketry and Bayonet Practice.	7M.
	21		Preparing of Training circuit 9 am – 10.30 Practice with Electricity & trench aids. 11.30 TO E.T. 2 – 3 PM Coy Rest. 1 Ch 4 hrs Insp.	M.
	22		O.C. Coy Lecture N.R. & W. Officers on BARRAGE FIRE. Morning spent without Lecture firing & care of Rifle men etc. 11 – 12.30 Ammunition. Action. 2 – 3 PM Musketry. (H.P. Practice (2. N)) & Lewis element. 2/ BEECHAM and parties. Arnchy perf. & 2 issues hearing on 7 am mitt at on parties & inst. on MINIATURE TRENCHES. S.E. of BUSSE 60 M. 2/27 GRIFFITHS i/c of party of their parties. 7 OR to hat. Parties of Training including 9 pm to 30 Lecture Pm 11 – 12.30 Foot pleases & clearing of firing. hat. 2/7 HIGHAM was in charge 4 ORs making packets en-hang MINIATURE trench. is in learning bag.	M.
	23		2/27 GENOVA pieces hand paper by Col. 2 OR to hat. stand parade. A.C. Smith NCOs 9 am C.S.G in a.s. Working hat. nine person by men 2/5 WALKINTON to the Afternoon 20 Ors on hat.	M.
	24		Sgd J. Tittle M.C.O. O.C. "I" Coy. 2/20 July 19th	

WAR DIARY or INTELLIGENCE SUMMARY.

Army Form C. 2118.

Place	Date	Hour	Summary of Events and Information	Remarks and references to Appendices
HALIFAX CAMP	JUNE 25		A practice Barrage with Divn in the morning witnessed by Lt Col H.C.O. & Lt Col 2i/c 26/6/17 G.O.C. We were relieved by teams of No 115 AE. CAMP 4th M.H.M.C.G. and remainder. When Employment Duties, Btllr on Instruction Lecture Duty and remainder. Attend 1. A SAA old crater saw an air fight at 9 a.m. C.O. Brig, & another party was wounded by shrapnel of his own — two LINDALE 2nd Lieut wounded. We on duty 5 stretcher cases. Sgt Wilson (Bmr Henry Sectn. wounded) 2nd Lieut Evans was injured by a lorry. Reinf. 9 W.Os. 9NCO apr. wen. Arrival of reinf. Warned up heavily which in the effective rate of fire fr, 3 Blr ratable C.B.W.O.C = No 3. There was a working party under 2/LT OENNIE and No 3 working party.	No 3. Copies
No 3.
No 3.
	26		Programme of Training included Gunnery Lectures Topography Afternoon for Gunnery parties. Gun Explanations was pitched to all of us regiment No 1 & No 3 section practice the usual unit positions. (Advance to New) IH- general training - (Advance to New) 1hr General time pur.	No 3.
	27		Programme of work inclusive A to 30 Barrage drill at Ar Green E.S. Relieve p No 2 section & No 4 section terminated the work and of gun fatigue. No 3 section & No 4 section retired from what brining the ritles.	No 3.
HALIFAX CAMP	28.		Morning Work included Gunnery & Rifle drill and Inspection of Harness & 3 PM. The C.O. was birthday lunch. The weather unchanged, much 2oz. retrieved 2/LT PILKINGTON was in charge of without Fort. Of 10 man recapture 2/LT PILKINGTON accompany re. O.C. 19 ZILLEBEKE to pay a certificate of (M.G.C. Section) accompany re. O.C. 19 ZILLEBEKE to pay a certificate 29/6/17- Hot weather in evening bath picture.	No 3.

Army Form C. 2118.

WAR DIARY
or
INTELLIGENCE SUMMARY.
(Erase heading not required.)

Instructions regarding War Diaries and Intelligence Summaries are contained in F.S. Regs., Part II. and the Staff Manual respectively. Title pages will be prepared in manuscript.

Place	Date	Hour	Summary of Events and Information	Remarks and references to Appendices
HALIFAX CAMP	JUNE 28.		In the afternoon O.C. Coy accompanied by 2/Lt HIGHAM arranged for relief of 22nd M.G Coy by us. in the line proceeding to their dispositions at YPRES & returning 4pm to Coy H.Q.	M.
	29		Section Reliefs:— Information for relief during afternoon. No.1 & No.2 Coy took over the dispositions of 22nd M.G. Coy (5) guns from 2.3 M.G. Coy Coy (5) No. 24 & No.6 Coy took over the dispositions of 22nd M.G. Coy (5) guns from 2.3 M.G. Coy Coy (5) accompanied by 2/Lt IVENONS proceeded by route march from YPRES Camp HALIFAX CAMP at 3.15pm. No.1 Section reached Coy H.Q at 6 p.m — No.2 Section 7 pm — No.3 Section 7 pm — No.4 Section 8 pm. No 4 Section arrived at Coy H.Q No 3 Section 11pm, in turn at 12 m.n.	R.O. 187. R.O. 182. No.4 Order (orders) Appendix "A"
			HALIFAX CAMP with transport dispositions Command of LT A.H. NEALE. Coy parades at 9 am. In spite of shelling of top communication trench the relief was completed by 11am 30.6.17. without casualties. Coy HQ "WRECKAGE" (in INFANTRY B'NS) YPRES —	
YPRES. TRENCHES.	30	3am	Gun positions:— No.1 Section 2 gun RLY WOOD 1gun LILLE GATE 1gun HELLFIRE CORNER No.2 Section 1 gun RIFLE F.M. 1 gun MENIN RD. 1.17.A.9.9. 2 gun W of Y WOOD. 8 gun of 21st M.G. Coy No.3 Section attached to 24th M.G. Coy 4 of their guns were engaged in A.A. work, & in night subsidiary attack 1 pm CHINA WALL, 1gun GORDON Ho, 1gun LEINSTER ST, 1gun REGENT ST — additional guns were:— 1 pm CHINA WALL, 1gun GORDON Ho, 1gun HALFWAY Ho respectively. SECTION DEPOTS of 24 and 218 M.G. Coys at RLY WOOD and Jnction of BEETTR and WESTLANE O.C. Coy visits guns in the line — Shelling of RLY and Jnction of Coy H.Q.	
		3pm — 6pm	YPRES heavily shelled including vicinity of Coy H.Q.	M.
		8.20 pm	O.C. Coy visits F.O.E H.Q.	
		10 P.M.	Relieving of infantry in line makes trump at school house — which was under heavy barrage fire at 11.30 p.m. 2nd Bay Transport & details moved from HALIFAX CAMP to TORONTO CAMP. forming Reserve of No. Bay Transport & details moved from HALIFAX CAMP to TORONTO CAMP. LT A.V. SULLY rejoined from G.H.Q. M.G. Course.	

War Diary
of the
24th M.G. Company
for the
Month of July 1917
by
Lieut F.J. Beechman.

Army Form C. 2118.

WAR DIARY
or
INTELLIGENCE SUMMARY.

(Erase heading not required.)

Instructions regarding War Diaries and Intelligence Summaries are contained in F. S. Regs., Part II. and the Staff Manual respectively. Title pages will be prepared in manuscript.

Place	Date	Hour	Summary of Events and Information	Remarks and references to Appendices
YPRES	July 2nd 1916	12.30am 3.15am	Enemy shelled WEST LANE with H.E. and GAS SHELLS. O.C. Company, accompanied by Lt F.G. HIGHAM visited gun in the and reworked barrage positions. Lieut SULLY relieved HIGHAM who returned to Company H.Q. On the following day YPRES was heavily shelled by guns of all calibres. MOMBRE CRATER was bombed with rifle grenades at intervals during the night the enemy sending VERY LIGHTS continuously from No 3 & No 4 CRATERS	7/B.
YPRES	2nd		YPRES & MUDLANE were shelled intermittently, though not as heavily, as on the previous day. The XIX Corps on our left carried out a counter-battery bombardment from 10pm till 12 M.N.	7/B.
	3rd		YPRES and the back area were heavily shelled between 12.30 and 1.30 a.m.	7/B.
		2am	75th Machine Gun Company completed a relief of the 21st Company in the sub-sector	

(A7093). Wt. W22850/M1293. 750,000. 1/17. D. D. & L., Ltd. Forms/C2118/14

WAR DIARY or INTELLIGENCE SUMMARY

Army Form C. 2118.

Place	Date	Hour	Summary of Events and Information	Remarks and references to Appendices
YPRES	July 3rd	4 am	C.C. Company reassembled by 2/Lt WALKINTON. Snipers gun on the line and returned at 7 am. Enemy A. planes were engaged by our Machine Gun fire at the following times 4.30am 5 am 5.15am 6.30am 8.30am 9am 12.30pm 5.30pm and 9 pm. No 4 Section (under 2/Lt WALKINTON) relieved No 2 Section (2/Lt BENNIE) the relief being completed by 11 am. It was	M/B
		12 MN	Lt BEECHMAN accompanied by C.S.M. selected site for S.A.A Dump at OUTPOST FARM. Lt CLANCHY Jones from M. G. Corps BASE, CAMIERS	No 9/93/14 under signature of Curran
"	4th		GAS SHELLS were fired into vicinity of the "SCHOOLHOUSE" at 3.30am. Enemy A. Planes were prominently active during the day	M/B
		11pm	Lt BEECHMAN met representative of the 2nd NORTHAMPTON REGT and 2 PLATOONS at HELLFIRE CORNER to convey S.A.A. to Point Company was continued until 2am when S/A.A. was camouflaged. Sgt Wells transferred to 221st Company to C.S.M.	

WAR DIARY
or
INTELLIGENCE SUMMARY.

(Erase heading not required.)

Army Form C. 2118.

Place	Date	Hour	Summary of Events and Information	Remarks and references to Appendices
YPRES	July 5th	4am	the Machine gun position in MUD LANE SAP was blown in and the Ram buried. There were no casualties except 1 case of shock. The gun remained in action. B.C Company recovered new Machine gun position near the junction of CAMBRIDGE ROAD and the RAILWAY will assist in covering "NO MANS LAND" in front of IDENTITY TR and 1 DISTTR. 1 Gun of No 1 Section was placed here.	M.
		5.45pm 10pm	YPRES shelled by guns of heavy calibre. Lt BEECHMAN met Officer & a platoon of 2nd NORTHAMPTONSHIRE REGt near HELLFIRE CORNER whence S.A.A. was conveyed to OUT POST FARM as on previous night & parts from the Company were detailed for this work and returned at 2am 6th inst.	
			2 O.R. to U.K leave. 1 O.R from leave. 1 O.R. wounded (shell shock)	
do.	6th	4am	O.C Company accompanied by 2nd Lt M.C.D. and B.C. 25th Machine Gun Company proceeded on a tour of inspection of the guns & returned at 6 am	M.

Army Form C. 2118.

WAR DIARY
or
INTELLIGENCE SUMMARY.

(Erase heading not required.)

Instructions regarding War Diaries and Intelligence Summaries are contained in F.S. Regs., Part II. and the Staff Manual respectively. Title pages will be prepared in manuscript.

Place	Date	Hour	Summary of Events and Information	Remarks and references to Appendices
YPRES	July 6th		There was low enemy activity during the day the 25th Machine Gun Company relieved the Company in the line on the night 6/7. This relief was complete by 8 am without casualties. The Company proceeding to MONTREAL CAMP.	B.D. 188 C.O.O. no 15 M/S
MONTREAL CAMP	7th		The vicinity was shelled with 8" shells during the night. 1 O.R. to rest camp. 2 O.R.s AA tower with no 4 Squadron R.F.C. ABEELE 2 O.R. reported to commander DOMINION CAMP with SAA Limber. 2 O.R. no 3 Section proceeded under order to BIRR CROSS ROADS to act as storemen at SAA dump. 1 O.R. to Hospital	B.O. no 173. ABEELE
		2 pm	Company moved to STEENBECQUE in buses. Marking & indexing point US.E of POPERINGHE on POP. CASSEL ROAD (UPS). The Company transport surveyed independently :- route ABEELE — STEENVOORDE — HAZEBROUCK — STEENBECQUE. Company billets at late place on night, entraining on the following day at 1:30 pm. for the BOMY area. Company transport moved independently starting at 10 am. The Company arrived at PETIGNY at 5 pm & listing & was billeted.	B.O. no 189. C.O.O. no 6.
	8th		B- HIGHAM having proceeded in advance	M/S
PETIGNY				

WAR DIARY
or
INTELLIGENCE SUMMARY.

Army Form C. 2118.

Place	Date	Hour	Summary of Events and Information	Remarks and references to Appendices
PETIGNY	JULY 8th		As on the previous day, ie billet the whole company, line transport & stores, were accommodated in quarters	
do	9th		A programme of training commenced; the programme included daily Parade 7-7.30am. Close Order Drill. 8 am Breakfast. 8-45am Section Officers 9 am C.O's Inspection 10-45am Section Officers Orderly Room 12-45pm Company Officers Orderly Room. 1st Training period 9-10.30am. 2nd Training Period 11 - 12-30 pm.	
		9-10.30 11-12.30pm	Programme for 9-7-17 Cleaning Gun Sect. Cleaning Disc. etc B.C. Company make clean all gun fits	
		2-3pm	O.C. 24th Inf. Bde visited the Company during the morning Instruction of Stannic Indirect fire Appliance	
do	10th	9-10.30 11-12.30 2-3pm	O.C. from Hospital Battery Drill Rapid Construction of Gun-pits Section Reliefs. O.C. Company make to Company transport	

WAR DIARY
or
INTELLIGENCE SUMMARY.

(Erase heading not required.)

Army Form C. 2118.

Place	Date	Hour	Summary of Events and Information	Remarks and references to Appendices
PETIGNY	JULY 10th		G.O.C. 24th Inf Bde visited Company H.Q.	M.
-do-	11th	9.10-30am 11-12.30 2-3pm	Battery Drill. Rapid construction of Gun-position Lecture Gases. 9.O.R Jones from Base Depot. 1 O.R. from Hospital	M.
-do-	12th	9.10 11-12.30 2-3pm	Battery Drill. Instruction Zero lines. Handling of Arms. 1 O.R. from leave.	M.
-do-	13th	9.10-15am 2-3pm	Battery Drill. Instruction subject "linking Gps. During the morning no Lectures to officers in a Scheme on the practice tactics between ERNY ST JULIEN and DELETTE. Battery Drill.	M.

Place	Date	Hour	Summary of Events and Information	Remarks and references to Appendices
PETIGNY	JULY 14th		MORNING: Cleaning guns etc & revision of technical equipment which J.O.C. 8th Division visited the Company during the afternoon & viewing the Company a practice scheme under Lt BEECHMAN while O.C. Company attended a machine gun conference at 8th Division H.Q. Scheme the assembly position was at HALFWAY HOUSE the Company formed in LEINSTER ST at 4:30pm ZERO HOUR was 6:15pm. 9 Battery (with 3 sections) under Lt SULLY & "L" Battery (with 2+4 sections) under Lt HIGHAM rested in Barrage Position near MENIN ROAD E of HOOGE and were ready to open fire at Z+15 mins. having started at Z+15 mins. the Transport Officer (Lt DEANS) supervised the formation of dumps and Lt BEECHMAN supervised the maintenance of intercommunication & report centres. Lieut Hunt to U.K. 14 days leave.	2h July Bde g 1143 g 0hr1.
	JULY 15th 1917		The scheme of the previous days was repeated the 23rd Inf Bde Company parades at 8am reaching	M/B. 8th Division w 1359/153 2:00am.

Army Form C. 2118.

WAR DIARY
or
INTELLIGENCE SUMMARY.
(Erase heading not required.)

Place	Date	Hour	Summary of Events and Information	Remarks and references to Appendices
PETIBUS	July 15"		The assembly area at 9.30 am or the occasion the Battery commenced from the N trans position to the 2nd S of WESTHOEK in JABBERT. Transport arrangements similar to those of the previous day. Visual signalling being used. O.C. Companies interviewed there operation which terminated at 1.15 pm. At 1.15 pm presentation of meal by O.C. II Corps took place in the training ground at which the 2nd & 24th Inf. Bdes. were present. This was followed by lecture to all the officers at COYECQUE at 5.30 pm. by G.O.C. II Corps. 20 O.R's H.N. leave.	M.B.
	7" 16		MORNING Battery drill & Care of Arms. AFTERNOON drawing of Gun Pits. there was a lecture for all officers at COYECQUE delivered by G.S.O.1. II Corps 3.30pm	M.
		5.30 PM	1 Sgt & 1 OR attended the demonstration of Jucken Sacks	

Army Form C. 2118.

WAR DIARY
or
INTELLIGENCE SUMMARY.
(Erase heading not required.)

Place	Date	Hour	Summary of Events and Information	Remarks and references to Appendices
PETIGNY	17th		Work on picture frames continued on Company parade ground. Place touched lecture at ERNY-ST JULIEN by O.C. 8th Division to Officers & Senior N.C.O's of the Brigade were present.	M3.
		4pm	O.C. Company attended a C.O. conference at Bde. H.Q.	
		2.oPP	Fell in U.T.M.	
	18th		Divisional Leisure Day	
		9am	Company parade. Company was formed up by O.C. Company [?] 1500 R was actually formed 2/Lieut Janois his Right) the programme laid for introduction in subsequent pages, to the Company arrangements came to a general relaxation.	M3. 8.00 ms
	19th		Company sports at Company H.Q.rs the 23rd M.G. Company 2/12th M.G. Company, 14th T.M. Battery participated in these sports and the 8th Divisional Band played the sports were followed by a prize giving & tea for visitors & competitors—	M3.

Army Form C. 2118.

WAR DIARY
or
INTELLIGENCE SUMMARY.
(Erase heading not required.)

Instructions regarding War Diaries and Intelligence
Summaries are contained in F. S. Regs., Part II.
and the Staff Manual respectively. Title pages
will be prepared in manuscript.

Place	Date	Hour	Summary of Events and Information	Remarks and references to Appendices
PETIGNY	20th		Cleaning kit & preparation for move	MB
do	21st		Company moved to LESPRESSES the time table was as follows:- 10 R to Hazebrouck	B.O. 191
		3.15am	Reveille	MB
		4.15am	Breakfast	
		4.55am	Company paraded & 24th T.M. Battery marched to one and the Company under 2 Lt Griffiths Lieut. BENNIE advance party under 2 Lt Griffiths proceeded ahead to billets at Butrieu-Route au BOIS	
LESPRESSES			- CUHEM = LIGNY-LES-AIRE - AUCHY=AUX-BOIS. 10 R 6 Hazebrouck	
	22nd		Company less Transport entrained at BERGUETTE. time of departure 9 am Q.O.R. under Lt SULLY acted as loading & Entraining party reaching BERGUETTE St at 8am, Lt HIGHAM guard commander after the loading party paraded at 8am, the memorial the company at 9am the Company transport moved with the Bde transport to CAESTRE & thence to the following day to CAMP N. C. 22.0.8.7 near BUSSEBOM Arriving 9am 23rd inst	B.O. 190. MB

WAR DIARY
or
INTELLIGENCE SUMMARY

Army Form C. 2118.

Place	Date	Hour	Summary of Events and Information	Remarks and references to Appendices
LESPRESSES	22nd		The Company turned at ABEELE 8TH at 2.30 pm the intruding party included the train in a lorry CAMP was reached at 5pm. Where billets were taken over. From the 19th M.G. Coy G.2.C.7.8	
BUSSEBOOM		6pm	O.C. Company visited Bde. H.Q.	
		11pm	Lt. BEECHMAN arranged details for taking over the guns from the 7th M.G. Company in the line. Three arrangements were however cancelled.	
		2.0pm	leave till	
do	23rd	9am	O.C. Company visited H.Q. 7th M.G. Company at YPRES. Arrangements by Lieut. HUTTON to arrange relief.	Ref 0.0.61 M. & S.Q
		7pm	C. Battery under Lt. SULLY relieved the 7th M.G. Company in the night sector. 4 guns were in position in BONDST, LEINSTERST, GORDON HOUSE, (HINMAN). (no. 5 listed) 4 guns (Battery) Belgian	C6009 2nd A. Bde BM 141
		8pm	Battery position near HELLFIRE CORNER. Its harassing fire the relief was completed without mishap. The night was spent in making & keeping good loopholes dealing with an improvised position. The heavy gas shelling during the night & prior to BEECHMAN proceeded to YPRES and established	

Army Form C. 2118.

WAR DIARY
or
INTELLIGENCE SUMMARY.
(Erase heading not required.)

Instructions regarding War Diaries and Intelligence Summaries are contained in F.S. Regs., Part II. and the Staff Manual respectively. Title pages will be prepared in manuscript.

Place	Date	Hour	Summary of Events and Information	Remarks and references to Appendices
YPRES	23rd		A H.Q Coy of the WRECKAGE party of 50 or under 2nd Lt Sowerby 2/Northamptonshire Regt reported for duty & carrying party and wiring attached to this Unit.	M.
			I.O.R. Lieut Barr Duket.	
YPRES WRECKAGE	24th	7 am	O.C. Company Wiriting party in the line returning to Company H.Q. at 1 am	M.
		10 pm	The 2" List Yorks Regt carried out a daylight raid leaving 14 prisoners May 23rd in 2d PILLY carried out interruption of the enemy supplies	
		10 pm	2nd Lt Journey & 2 L.O.R reported at HALFWAY HOUSE 2 "L" Battery & details moved to HALIFAX CAMP	
			I.O R. Lieut to O.R. I.O R. to Holpard	
	25th	2.00 4 am	Enemy fired Gas shells in YPRES	M.
		5 am	B Company finished its line returning at 9.15am	
		10.15	C Company visited Bn H.Q. at HALFWAY HOUSE	
			Transfer Above to DOMINION CAMP D.M.G.O. "L" Battery moved from Halifax & Colette.	
		8pm		

WAR DIARY or INTELLIGENCE SUMMARY

Army Form C. 2118.

Place	Date	Hour	Summary of Events and Information	Remarks and references to Appendices
YPRES WEIGHT CRANGE	July 25		HALIFAX CAMP to HALFWAY HOUSE Company & 12 M.N. this party was ordered ahead of MOATED GRANGE at 6.45 am up Group of Rail-heads and down near MOATED GRANGE	M
		8.3pm	OC Company proceeded to HALFWAY HOUSE to supervise the disposition of the guns. These were as follows:- No 1 Section 4 Guns Support position SE of HELLFIRE CORNER No 2 Section, 2 Guns no 1 Locker, 2 guns No 3 Section in trolley position near GORDON HOUSE outside LEINSTER TR 1 Gun LEINSTER, 1 Gun BOND ST No 4 Section 2 Guns No 3 Section in reserve at HALFWAY HOUSE ready to reinforce any of these dispositions who might become casualties. Guns of ZOUAVE WOOD West entrance. The object of these dispositions, though not anticipated, though its repel an attack which was anticipated, though it did not actually occur. 2/Lt RILL wounded 2 OR wounded	
-do-	26th	6am	OC Company returned to Company Hd Qrs.	
		11am	Lt BEECHAM visited the guns in the line returning at 3pm	M
		4pm	OC Company proceeded to HALFWAY HOUSE where he took up his Hd Qrs	
HALFWAY HOUSE		11pm	2/Lt SULLY returned to Company Hd Qrs at YPRES during the night barrage	

WAR DIARY or INTELLIGENCE SUMMARY.

Army Form C. 2118.

Place	Date	Hour	Summary of Events and Information	Remarks and references to Appendices
YPRES. WIEKTJE & HALFWAY HOUSE	JULY 26		Fire was carried out on the BELLEWAARDE RIDGE by way of co-operation with a feint. Artillery average 11,000 rounds fired. 8 guns actively by mounties on SOS lines. 2 OR wounded. 2 OR went to H. H.	M.
	27th		During 15 post Ouistiti the wire was artillery fire on either side in the morning. Although it became normal later in the day. No 3 section under Lt- BENNIE proceeded to rear company this on relief. No 1 section remained in reserve.	M.
	28th	5-15	4 guns No 2 Sec carried out indirect fire on the BELLE WARRDE RIDGE in support of a raid. 6,000 rounds were fired. The guns of No 2 Section were laid on SOS lines during the night.	M.
	1pm		During the day Corporal M. J. M. L. & R. J. Section 12,000 rounds fired. No it retaliated & hit caused but by this 15th Division. Were reply being. IGUANA SWITCH & SUPPORT and WOOD W. of RED LODGE. Section was during heavy shell attack. Lt. fatally wound & Lt. RITZ DUGOUT from HALFWAY HOUSE. Lt. SULLY wound from near Company HQ. 2 OR to Hospital. 2 OR Wounded.	

Army Form C. 2118.

WAR DIARY
or
INTELLIGENCE SUMMARY.
(Erase heading not required.)

Instructions regarding War Diaries and Intelligence Summaries are contained in F. S. Regs., Part II. and the Staff Manual respectively. Title pages will be prepared in manuscript.

Place	Date	Hour	Summary of Events and Information	Remarks and references to Appendices
YPRES RAMPARTS at HALFWAY HOUSE	1917 29th		Carrying party proceeded to YPRES where they were eventually withdrawn. From 6pm to 8.30pm our Artillery carried on a heavy Bombardment, all guns were laid on S.O.S. lines during the day but at night no 2 section commenced its usual harassing fire. The guns were located as being to heavily retaliation were obliged to cease fire. 1,000 rounds fired. Casualties Lieut Stevens killed.	M
	30th		No 1 & 3 sections with the majority of company Hd Qrs of the Coy park'd in YPRES at 8 pm Running of company Hd Qrs at HALFWAY HOUSE at 9 pm.	M.S.
HODGE	31st	11p	At 11.30pm Nos 1,2 & 3 sections formed up complete and carried one dt kit machine holes surrounds the remains of HALFWAY HOUSE at 12 MN they advanced to their recently dug Iulirid ZOUBYE WOOD No 4 Section and 2 guns to defensive positions on road E of HALFWAY HOUSE and 2 Lt WALKINGTON with the remainder advanced to form up well N of Hun Rd in shell holes in front of KINGSWAY SUPPORT there his guns advanced with the 1st Wave of attack, just after ZERO hour and 2/Lt WALKINTON was hit by a piece of shell 600 yds after we have forward & began	

WAR DIARY or INTELLIGENCE SUMMARY

Army Form C. 2118.

Place	Date	Hour	Summary of Events and Information	Remarks and references to Appendices
HODGE	Sept	4.30 am	No. 1 & 3 Sections ("B" Battery) under no. 1 Lieut. ("B" Battery) advanced towards HODGE in the region of KINGSWAY SUPPORT eventually reaching pieces E of HODGE. Casualties owing to heavy enemy barrage were heavy. Altogether into two In dark to get the weak spots in the enemy lines and the line was to try to manoeuvre them. The infantry were held up near the entrance of the tunnel. The same on the Sherway fired & and nothing could be done while the enemy were Metalgate this was special effect under ZERO then	JW
		5·50am	the first Barrage was opened. All firing was within chests and second Barrage fired and came late. S.O.S. line. The Co. & Co. operators arrived at the battery positions soon after and were followed by D pack convoy of 19 animals under Lt. DEANS who had moved his transport under the bank to BELGIAN BATTERY CORNER at 3 am.	
		6 am	It then became evident that the situation on my right had been difficult up and it was decided to form a defensive flank to cope with this situation, the Battery advanced under Corpl PRATT to JAMES TR. through CHATEAU WOOD. Some casualties being	

WAR DIARY or INTELLIGENCE SUMMARY

Army Form C. 2118.

(Erase heading not required.)

Place	Date	Hour	Summary of Events and Information	Remarks and references to Appendices
JAMES TR CHATEAU N60D			returned en route from RUDKIN Shelling which had shortened during that was now resumed. Lieut. NOTT ASKEW who were reinforced highly arrived in support of the two defensive guns and hastily formed numerous thrown across the entrance from the rly. bank flying specially Lewis Gun guns were placed on FNOH's 4/J.55 and white and on BELLEWAARDE RIDGE. Lt. BEECHMAN had established communications first by visual signalment, by some with the outposts on Rte. fly Qrs. and was in touch with the Bde. Staff throughout the action. He was for one command of No. 4 licton (4 guns) which formed the left flank of the defences. The defences were maintained and compy. now had little scarcely the fire the enemy M.Gs. was answered fire by fly Qtrs for the rifle gun. Company fire Qrs. were established in a MG dugout in JAMES TR.	
		8 am.	with rations Lts etc. an S.A.A. arrived in the afternoon and further S.A.A. was brought up by carrying party under 2/Lt. LIVESAY, Q reserve of guns was formed and held in readiness at Company HQrs. At 12.30pm the positions of the guns of No. 4 licton were	

WAR DIARY
or
INTELLIGENCE SUMMARY.

(Erase heading not required.)

Army Form C. 2118.

Place	Date	Hour	Summary of Events and Information	Remarks and references to Appendices
CHATEAU WOOD	JULY 13th		Spotlights altered to meet of new Star & counter-attack zone in frying from the immediate front and two guns of No 2 Lichen Keep up fixture to the western end of JABBER AVENUE. 6 8 6/17/ J Newman Lt OT for O.C. 24 M.G. Coy.	

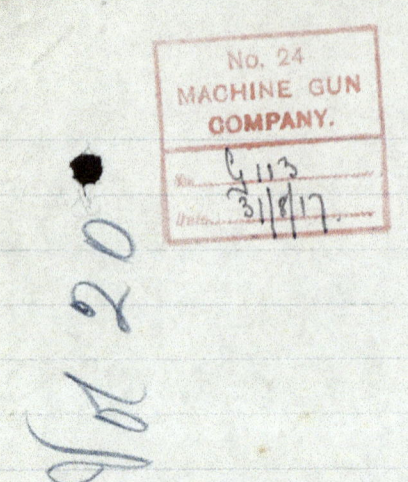

Vol 20

War Diary of the
24TH Machine Gun Company
for the month of
August 1917
by
Lieut A G Sully for
Officer Commanding.

Wt. W12885/M1307. 40,000 pads 2.17. J. T. & S., Ltd. Army Form **C348** (Pads).

MEMORANDUM.

No. 24
MACHINE GUN
COMPANY.
G113
31/8/17

August 31st 1917

From   O.C. 24TH M.G. Company

To   D.A.G. Base

Herewith War Diary of the 24TH M.G. Company, for the month of August 1917.

A. Victor Sucley Lieut
for O.C. 24TH M.G. Coy

Army Form C. 2118.

WAR DIARY
or
INTELLIGENCE SUMMARY.

(Erase heading not required.)

Instructions regarding War Diaries and Intelligence Summaries are contained in F.S. Regs., Part II and the Staff Manual respectively. Title pages will be prepared in manuscript.

Place	Date	Hour	Summary of Events and Information	Remarks and references to Appendices
JAMES TRENCH (CHATEAU WOOD)	AUGUST 1st	5am	The night was quiet. As was the early morning, it is 5am when the Enemy shelled Chateau Wood and forward areas again. Officers of the relieving Company, No 7 M.G. Coy, 25 Division	
		7pm	arrived in the morning and relief was complete. By about 7 pm. Coy had carried Gun Kits to Halfway Ho. where transport was waiting. Company then proceeded to quarters at	
MONTREAL CAMP	2nd	9am	Roll call was held at 9am and shewed (Return for July 25 & August 1) KILLED - ORs 4. WOUNDED:- Officers 4; ORs 25. MISSING:- ORs 2. Cleaning up of Parades. No 2 Section was	
	3rd		return Burial No 3, and No 3 Return Guns No 2. O.C. Coy, Lt Higham & Lt Sully with a party of approximately 20 NCO's then marched Devonshire Cp to met GOC 8th Division at 10am. Remainder of Coy on cleaning-up of Guns sent to Ordnance for overhaul. Six or seven gun mountings reported.	
(LE TEMPLE now) STEENVOORDE	4th		Coy embussed near quarters at 9.30am and moved via Vlamertinghe, Poperinghe & Abeele to C.Roats NW of Steenvoorde. Quarters not very good. 1 OR to Hospital.	
	5th		Coy paraded at 9am & marched to Parade ground of 2nd East Lancashire Regt & was addressed by G.O.C. IId Corps.	
	6th		Training and Cleaning of Parades. The reward 5 overhauled guns arrived from Ordnance. 1 OR from Hospital.	
	7th		Lt F.J. Beechman proceeded to join No 23 M.G. Coy as 2nd in Command & AU Swan took over duties of 2nd in Command to Company. Six remaining guns sent to Ordnance for overhaul. Short route march in morning followed by Inspection of Gun Kit by O.C. Coy. Lt Deans (wounded on leave of absence) GUK Lt Higham took over transport. temporarily. Transport inspected by B.T.O. "P" Battery in thereafter. Renown as A Battery (182 Big.) and "L" Batteries R Battery (3rd section)	
	8th		2/Lt Griffiths attended F.G.C.M. on Pte Dermody (S.I. Wound) as President at H.Q. 15th Worcestershire Regt. Coy Rolled 7.30 to 9.0am at Battle Division as Battle Steenvoorde T.O.E.T. & Cleaning of Kit. 1 OR from Hospital.60	

Army Form C. 2118.

WAR DIARY
or
INTELLIGENCE SUMMARY.
(Erase heading not required.)

Instructions regarding War Diaries and Intelligence Summaries are contained in F. S. Regs., Part II. and the Staff Manual respectively. Title pages will be prepared in manuscript.

Place	Date	Hour	Summary of Events and Information	Remarks and references to Appendices
(LE TOUQUET No) STEENVOORDE	August 1917 9th 10th 11th		Short Route march C and squad drill. Squad drill and training parades as usual. Gun Rifle cleaned and timber oiled. Training parades as usual. Squad drill and training parades as usual, A/O.C 24th Brigade addressed officers & sergeants	
	12th		Lecture by O.C. Coy and Battery Commanders on use of C Emergale dials. Practical training in Bayonet demonstration of firing of signal rockets.	
	13th		4 Officers reinforcements joined from 38th Divisional Reinforcement Battalion. 2/Lt C.P. Smith, 2/Lt Cappart, 2/Lt A.H. Weaver	
HALIFAX CAMP	14th	4 a.m	Reveillé 4.0 a.m Coy moved off at 7 a.m. via Steenvoorde Abeele Reninghelst 2 Ouderdom to Halifax Camp by Motor Route. One new was carried part of the way in the Mess Cart. At 4 p.m Lt Sully, 2/Lt Griffiths & 2/Lt Smith with 1 NCOS moved for section proceeded to Birr X Roads and ponce after receiving instruction from Major	
		6 p.m	M.O.O. D.M.G.O. formed a dump of S.A.A. at Lake Farm, a carrying party being supplied by 1st Sherwood Foresters. It was info: sable on account of the	
		11 p.m	conf Gala darkness of the night to accounts the Battery position followed	
	15th	2 a.m	to camp at 2 a.m. Belt-feeding during Cannoning. B Battery under Lt Sully paraded ready to move	
RED LODGE (WESTHOEK)		2.30 p.m	at 2.30 p.m and moved via BAB track and Ypres to Birr X Roads. 2/Lt Griffiths and Sgt Baxter preceded the Battery and formed a Coy's dump of S.A.A. at Battery position reached by O.C. Coy N of Red Lodge. B Battery carried up to Battery position	
		6 p.m	arriving about 6 p.m. Positions were dug just to the night of a German M.G. dugout. Carrying parties under 2/Lt Smith brought up 8 tins water and 3 boxes	
	16th		of Groot boxes & gun to above were spotted by the enemy and heavily shelled during	
		4.45am	Early cannoning and at 1.0 were after zero 3.0.R to that 2/W. Yorks & 2/Devons attacked the Green Line. Our artillery	

Army Form C. 2118.

WAR DIARY
or
INTELLIGENCE SUMMARY
(Erase heading not required.)

Instructions regarding War Diaries and Intelligence Summaries are contained in F. S. Regs., Part II. and the Staff Manual respectively. Title pages will be prepared in manuscript.

Place	Date	Hour	Summary of Events and Information	Remarks and references to Appendices
RED LODGE (WESTHOEK)	August 17th 16th	4.45am	Barrage was excellent. B. Battery fired on Ce HANEBEEK from 3gms (100 3'+ 20 minute and effect to beyond greetings from 3+20 minute (5 3'+1 hour 25 minute Positions continued to be easily observed by 5.9". One m.g was completely destroyed and one put out of action owing to a Round Barrel and broken muzzle-cap. Battery moved to a position 100yds left of M-9	
		6.10am	dugout. Reference ……… and fired on SOS lines when called for at	
		9.0am, 3.10pm & 9pm	9.0am, 9.45am 3.10pm & 9pm 2/Lt GRIFFITHS acted as F.O.O. at Kit 2Kat during Case of e.alions 3 range guns, two tripods and a dozen men arrived to man same about 12 noon	
	17 – 18th		Guns remained in position till mid-day 18th and were laid on Barrage lines just E of de HANEBEEK. Casualties Killed :- 2 ORs Wounded:- 1 Officer, 2/Lt CAPPEN 9 ORs. On relief of the Division by the 47th (London Territorial) Division the Battery withdrew. Shunting Pit made a grave at RIER X ROADS. Lt SWAIN CHATEAU dug-outs. O.C's neo-shire of the action is attached. Lt NEALE rejoined from leave. Reliefs were sent for to SWAN CHATEAU and the Coy moved off to HALIFAX CAMP at 5.30 pm. after inspection at 11 am. Accommodation good as before	O.C's Narrative attached.
SWAN CHATEAU				
HALIFAX CAMP	19th 20th		Company paraded for Protection at 9am. Subsequent or road outside Billet at 2.30pm. Busses moved via VLAMERTINGHE POPERINGHE ABEELE STEENVOORDE &	
LA BRIARDE (GENRE AREA B)			ST SILVESTRE CAPELLE to LA BRIARDE X ROADS. Billets sufficient for officers. Draft of 42 ORs, 2 2 officers 2/Lt E.T.BRUCE 2 2/Lt E.A. SKINNER joined from Reinforcement Battalion. Lt. DEANS rejoined from leave.	

(A7091) Wt. W12830/M1293. 750,000. 1/17. D. D. & L., Ltd. Forms/C.2118/14.

WAR DIARY
INTELLIGENCE SUMMARY.

(Erase heading not required.)

Army Form C. 2118.

Place	Date	Hour	Summary of Events and Information	Remarks and references to Appendices
LA BRIARDE (CAESTRE AREA B)	August 17 21st		Cleaning up Parade. GenGas Classes and also Divisional Inspection by F.M. Sir Douglas Haig near Rubli. The Company was congratulated on an exceedingly smart turn-out. Draft of 33 O.R's joined from Base at MICHAM.	
	22nd		Proceeded on leave to U.K. 1 O.R. from Hospital. Parades for training. Baths parade at STAPLE at 12 noon. All guns to field but in Coat action overhauled at Ordnance	
	23rd		Training Parades. T.O.E.T., signalling, & 2 thorough inspection of all gun Pt & spare parts. O.C. Coy proceeded on leave to U.K. 2 O.R. to Hospital.	
	24th		Physical training parade and inspection of gas affairs. Column, nature & training of Gunners & afterwards. 2 OR to Hospital.	
	25th		O.C. Coy visited trenches in afternoon. Various training parades including Relief on Barrage 2 & indirect fire by Section & Battery Commanders. 1 OR from Hospital	
	26th		Church Parade at 11 am & Café and at 9.30 & R.C. Limbers packed ready for move up the line	
	27-28 12.30am		Rod 6.00.1e 12.30 am Parade 2.30 am Company Gun Guard at 3 am and proceeded via GEORGE FLÊTRE, METEREN & BAILLEUL to LE ROHARIN 2/Lt WEAVER 2/Lt SKINNER No3 (reserve) Section of CMS (Sgt WALFORD) and details (Proceeded (5 months non NEUVE EGLISE. Remainder of Coy. 13.0. O.C Coy (Lt NEALE) and 2.0 in Command (at SULLY) proceeded (5 advanced H.Q. St YVES. (PLOEGSTEERT WOOD) to Care guides of the 1st N.Z.M.G. Coy were met and Relief was carried out Relief was complete	
ST YVES (PLOEGSTEERT Wd)		10 am	By 10.a.m. No 1 Section (2/Lt SMITH) in front on left. No 4 Section (2/Lt BRUCE) in	

WAR DIARY
INTELLIGENCE SUMMARY

Place	Date	Hour	Summary of Events and Information	Remarks and references to Appendices
ST YVES (PLOEGSTEERT WOOD)	August 27th	11 a.m.	Front on Right and No 2 Section (2/Lt GRIFFITHS) in support – C.o.a. (sic) Bavage and SO2 Guns were taken over. Sorry returned with carrying party (5 NCOs) Bavage 4 men per gun in trenches, plus NCOs two AA guns now HQ. Guns mounted at new HQ. 2/Lt SKINNER reconnoitred route to trenches.	
		5 p.m.	Spun it with rations, wind calm, arrived CAL. Very heavy rain & high wind. O.C. Coy visited gun positions. 800 rounds fired on Telephone & Orange Cy B4 section.	
	28th		AA positions. Guide for gun mounted on 27th. Loc.Lt. G5 N.C.O's on Raft Reference and Contains Coy 2/Lt SKINNER at 11.30 am. Transport fatigue & outside at Rear HQ. O.C. Coy visited guns and returned to Rear HQ at 4 p.m. Bavage 2/Lt GRIFFITHS, 2/Lt BRUCE, 1 sergeant, 2 signallers & 2 runners at Adv HQ. Both our own and the enemy's Troops and Artillery were fairly peaceful in this sector. No undue activity of any description. No. 1 Recon reported No. 4 Section fired 750 rounds at enemy crossroads. No. 2 section fired 3000 rounds into DEÛLÉMONT VILLAGE, and cuts roads & trenches in enemy territory. 1 OR from Hospital.	
PLOEGSTEERT Wd.	29th		Inspection Parade at 9 a.m. and fatigue on Transport till 11 a.m. at 2 p.m. OC Coy 2 2/Lt SKINNER visited guns Right firing Coy Nos 1, 2, 24 Sections	
	30th		1750 rounds were fired into WARNETON & DEÛLÉMONT. O.C. Coy visited trenches with DMGO & CMGO Woolleat, lightly Cotter No 3 Section – 2/Lt SKINNER – 2 spare men Rafc near HQ at 2.30 pm to release No 1 Section 2 teams of No 2 24 Section, about 10 spare men per section	

Army Form C. 2118.

WAR DIARY
or
INTELLIGENCE SUMMARY.
(Erase heading not required.)

Instructions regarding War Diaries and Intelligence Summaries are contained in F. S. Regs., Part II. and the Staff Manual respectively. Title pages will be prepared in manuscript.

Place	Date	Hour	Summary of Events and Information	Remarks and references to Appendices
ROEGSTEERT WOOD	August 30th		Going out of the line. Relief completed 6 p.m. No 4 Section handed over 4 gun position to 25th Coy; 2 romoured in rest at Coy HQ. Enemy artillery fire fairly more active 2 m.gs fired on our emp. Beeuwark at FLATTENED FARM. Enemy anti-aircraft firing was carried out. O.C. Coy returned 11 p.m.	
	31st		Second in Command visited Heincke at 12 noon. Details at Coy HQ. Relief at PAPOT. O.C. Coy visited Cina at 4 p.m. No 4 Section relieved 4 guns of No 13 AM Coy south of the rio en Doute. One gun of No 2 Section was relieved at a new position by a gun of No 21B Coy and took up a position first N of the SUGAR REFINERY, LA BASSE VILLE 15 en Garde Route of R'LY'S Relief complete 2 a.m. 1000 rounds anti aircraft fire during the day. No 3 section claim to have brought down an enemy aeroplane at 7.30 p.m; claim not yet substantiated 500 rounds indirect fired on WARNETON BRIDGE. Enemy artillery and m-g fire normal, aircraft slightly more active 1 or from Hostile	

From

    O.C. 24th Machine Gun Company.

To

    D.M.G.O. 8th. Division.

                    Ref. Map BELGIUM Sh.28 N.E. 1/20000.
Herewith report on the action of the 24th. M.G.Coy.
during the operations of the 16th. Aug. 1917.

             The tasks allotted to the Company were----
(1). From Zero - Zero + 20 to place barrage on the
ridge from J.3.A.23. - D.26.D.74. to cover the
advance to the GREEN LINE.
(2). From Zero + 20 - Zero + 85 to barrage to
cover the advance to & the consolidation of the
GREEN LINE. Barrage to be placed from D.27.D.92. to
D.27.B33.
(3). To remain on S. O. S. lines to open fire on
D.27.A98. - D.27D.92.
(4). To be prepared to put special S. O. S. on
North edge of POLYGON WOOD.

             The battery site as reconnoitred by the
O.C. on the 15th. inst. Owing to the conformation
of the ground, it was impossible to clear KIT & KAT
and the WESTHOEK RIDGE from the slope, so a position
on the low ridge near RED LODGE was chosen. The
battery arrived at 6.P.M., and dug in at J.X. C.61.
S.A.A. was brought up by a carrying party of
1. Officer & 50 O.R. (1st. Sherwood Foresters) and by
the spare numbers from the gun teams during the
night 15/16th. 2nd. Lt.C. P. Smith did good work
with this party, and succeeded in forming a dump
of 140,000 rounds before Zero hour. A further
50,000 rounds were subsequently fetched during
Z day as the unexpected expenditure threatened to
exhaust this dump.

             At Zero fire was opened. The enemy barrage
came down very promptly and one battery of 5.9s
heavily shelled the gun positions. Fire was maintained
until Zero + 85 when I ordered the teams still in
action to abandon the position, and to dig in for
the S. O. S. fire 100 further North at J.1 C.5.
The Nos.1 behaved splendidly during the period of
barrage fire, and continued firing throughout in
spite of the heavy shells falling practically on the
emplacements. Five guns were buried during this
period, two of which were destroyed, one damaged but
easily repaired two not damaged. I wish especially

to commend L/Cpl Sellars, No.72766, for his courage and devotion to duty, both at this time and subsequently when in charge of carrying parties. Lieut. A.V.Sully displayed conspicuous bravery, inconstantly passing from one gun position to another, checking elevation with a clinometer. 2nd. Lt. C. A. Pratt and eight O.R. became casualties. I attribute the small number of casualties mainly to the soft nature the ground, which prevented fragments and localised the destructive power of the shells. The teams had dug in deeply and a direct hit was needed to inflict harm.

After leaving the first position the teams dug in again and guns were laid on S. O. S. lines. Two of the four guns that I had been unable to man were brought from YPRES to replace those destroyed. Direction gave very little difficulty as the buildings on the crest gave the exact line. Elevation was maintained by running up the tangent sight until the line of sight cut the top of KIT & KAT. Belt-filling was simplified by having a large reserve of belt- boxes at hand. A small trench dug in behind a German concrete dug-out afforded shelter for spare Numbers for belt filling. At 8-30 A.M. I visited my F.O.O. 2nd. Lt. C. Griffiths, who reported that all had gone very well & that the GREEN LINE was in our hands. At 9.A.M. I received a message from him stating that there was considerable enemy activity on the North edge POLYGON WOOD. I accordingly switched all guns to the special S. O. S. and opened fire.

Rapid fire was maintained on POLYGON WOOD until 9-45. A.M., when I received a message saying that parties of the enemy were advancing from the ANZAC CREST on our own front. I accordingly switched guns on to our S. O. S. lines and continued fire for 2½ hours. The situation then had seemed to have cleared, and I received a message from the D.M.G.O. to report to the 23rd. I.B. H.Q. The F.O.O. reported that there were none of our troops East of the HANEBEEK R. so guns were relaid on the ANZAC CREST, and ordered to await a further S.O.S.

At 23rd. Brigade's H. Qtrs I was ordered to be prepared to place a barrage on this crest, as reports came in that we were still holding a few shell-holes East of the HANEBEEK. At 3-10 P.M. the SoS was sent up. Fire was immediately opened & maintained until 4-30 P.M., when the F.O. O. reported all quiet. During this period the enemy shelled heavily our old battery position and then in every emplacement except one.

During the evening new positions were strengthened. Oil as running very short. The CQMS who arrived with the rations sent some up and a further supply was obtained through the D.M.G.O. from the 25th. Coy.

Orders were received from the D.M.G.O. that the 25th Brigade were apparently without machine gun support, and that our SOS lines would be from J.2.B.32. to J.2. D.90. to cover their front. At about 9-0 P.M. the German SOS went up and his barrage fell. Our SOS went up and fire was reopened. For an hour every gun in the line appeared to be firing. It grew quieter about 10.P.M. and we ceased fire.

A German concrete dug-out that had been Cleared, served to rest the Nos. 1. who had been firing for long periods throughout the day and also to overhaul the guns. New barrels were fitted and all belt boxes were refilled ready for the dawn. No action developed however, and guns remained awaiting the SOS. until relieved the 47th. Division on the 18th.

As a result of experiences on the 31st July and the 16th. Aug. I beg to submit the following Conclusions.

(1). A cheaper form of belt is necessary. A very large wastage of belts has occurred on both occasions and much time has been lost in refilling.

(2). One section per company should be at the disposal of a competent Officer as a battery of opportunity. He should endeavour to occupy commanding positions and and engage targets by direct fire. The guns sent forward have followed the infantry too closely for this and valuable opportunities have been lost.

(3). It is extremely important that successive rallying points or report centres be fixed before the battle, or teams will be lost and individuals will become separated and non-effective.

(4). That much of the value of a carrying party is lost, unless the members of it know the company, the NCOs. under whose command they will come and the Officers to whom they are attached. The company patch should also be worn on the yellow armlet.

(5) That direct communication should be established between the company and the D.W. G.O. and that for this purpose signallers should be attached to him.

(6). The gun itself is extremely vulnerable to shrapnel or bullets. A divisional reserve of guns at a convenient central position would enable companies to carry on throughout.

(7). That a proportion of Officers and NCOs be trained in forward observation.

Capt.

August 22nd. 1917. O.C. 24th. Machine Gun Company.

Lt.Col. R.H. Nedet

2 Div Signals
Aldershot.
26 Oct 1937.

Dear Yule,

Here are two more maps of the WARNETON - PLOEGSTEERT area period Aug 19-26. 1917. My Company. 24th M.G. Coy 8th Div. took over from a New Zealand Brigade, after their successful attack.

We did a lot of work on our Gun positions and when

we had finished we had a critical visit from Hunter-Weston, (Corps Commander).

I remember the area well, points of intersection for fixing gun positions etc., my dugout was blown up the last night we were there.

Yours

Rupert Neale.

Recieved from
Lt.Col. R.H. Neale, Royal Signals.
27/10/37   2nd Divisional Signals

WAR DIARY

24TH MACHINE GUN COMPANY

FOR THE MONTH OF

SEPTEMBER
1917

By.

[signature] CAPT.
Commanding
24th M.G. Coy.

WAR DIARY
or
INTELLIGENCE SUMMARY.
(Erase heading not required.)

Army Form C. 2118.

Place	Date	Hour	Summary of Events and Information	Remarks and references to Appendices
LEINSTER RD NEUVE EGLISE T.21.B.85.5	Sept 1st		Weather unsettled. The neighbourhood of advanced Coy HQ at ST YVES was shelled with Gas Shells about 11 PM. Enemy Aircraft active taking smoke over our lines. (Support trenches) One of our Emm positions at U.16.B.8.3 was exploded by a Hostile MG. New emplacement commenced in.	
	2nd		Intermittent shelling by the Enemy throughout the day, particularly in the DOUVE VALLEY. Hostile Aircraft was particularly active. Squadrons flying over our line just before dusk and at 10.30pm several bombs were dropped in our back areas. Enemy aircraft slightly improved during the day. Details of Coy HQ attended a C of E Service at 9-30 AM conducted by Rev. Baines CF. Rev Highnam returned from leave. Rifleman Silly went on leave to U.K. No 4 Section relieved by No 1 Section already in the line.	
	3rd		Relieved Rein of the teams of 2 + 3 Sections already in the line. The Enemy shelled our Emm Positions at U.10.A.40 & 8 about 6.15 AM & the region of MOATED GRANGE for short periods during the day. Hostile Aircraft was very active throughout the day + this took place fire bombed during the evening. The weather was fine.	
	4th		Our machine guns fired on Hostile Aeroplanes which flew over our line in response to which the Enemy's Artillery & Machine Gun fire was directed on Kant Emm Positions at U.11.C & burned one of the Emms + 3 of a team.	

(A7992) Wt. W2839/M1293 750,000. 1/17. D. D. & L., Ltd. Forms/C.2118/4.

WAR DIARY
or
INTELLIGENCE SUMMARY

Army Form C. 2118.

Place	Date	Hour	Summary of Events and Information	Remarks and references to Appendices
KINSTER RD & Kalla NEUVE EGLISE SECT. T.21.B.15.y.5	4th		The Camerons Coy. carried North Aircraft was very active. At the request of the O.C. Battalion in the line. Very little Machine Gun fire was carried out. The weather was brilliantly fine & wind North Westerly	
	5th		Work at Coy H.Qrs proceeded with the ordinary training. 2.O.R. to Hospital. Only intermittent shelling occurred. Advanced by H.Qrs receiving most attention. Hostile Aircraft were very busy. Many of Hers over our lines at low altitudes. Capt. PRATT returned from leave to U.K.	
	6th		Work at Coy H.Qrs carried out ordinary programme of training regarded the Ammonal dumps at 12 Noon. The front was quiet with the exception of intermittent shelling. Battn area was again bombed by Hostile Aeroplanes west of NEUVE EGLISE.	
	7th		No 2 Section was relieved by No. 4 Section in the front line by Midnight. By 1 P.M. Our forward Gun position at the SUGAR REFINERY LA BASSE VILLE was heavily shelled with Gas Shells. Hostile Artillery was more active than usual. LA POTTERIE FARM, DOUVE VALLEY, CHASSEUR CABARET, LA BASSE VILLE being shelled at different periods. Relief was completed by 11 P.M.	

WAR DIARY or INTELLIGENCE SUMMARY

Army Form C. 2118.

Place	Date	Hour	Summary of Events and Information	Remarks and references to Appendices
LE INCTER M NEUF EGLISE T.21.B.15/75	Sept 8th		5. O.R.s to hospital re. L/Cpl Palmer 7/4 of the team which had been posted at the SUGAR REFINERY suffering from the effects of the gas shelling. Screens of the two retreat accompanied by violent vomiting and the prominent symptoms. At 11-10 A.m. Gas was discharged by trench mortars on to the village of WARNETON. In accordance with previously made arrangements L/Higham 7/4 of this position at the SUGAR REFINERY rather misfortunes were made to prevent the Enemy rushing our line which had been temporarily evacuated during the discharge of our Gas. In retaliation for this the Enemy dropped an Artillery Barrage on our front line for a short time. About midnight 8/9 a salvo shelled the Eastern fringe of PLOEGSTEERT WOOD And intercepted message from the Enemy trenches suggested the possibility of a Raid on our SECTOR. Accordingly arrangements were made for an Instant Smoke on S.O.S. lines to stem the barrage immediately Artillery started a Barrage on our front. Nothing however happened. Our wire cutting was carried out from a collated position on to a new Enemy work in front of UNCLEAN TRENCH 1500 rounds were fired from midnight 6 to 4.30 am on 9th Sept. The weather was fine.	

Army Form C. 2118.

WAR DIARY
or
INTELLIGENCE SUMMARY.

(Erase heading not required.)

Place	Date	Hour	Summary of Events and Information	Remarks and references to Appendices
LEINSTER Rd Sept NEUVE EGLISE T21 B 15 y 5	9		Starts at Coy H.Qrs paraded at 9.30 A.m for Aeroid Service at PLOEGSTEERT WOOD & DOUVE VALLEY was again shelled today the latter particularly at 9 P.M. Hostile Aeroplanes flew over our line at a low altitude being apparently driven off by Machine Gun fire. Indirect Overhead fire to the Enemys network was carried out from Midnight	
	10th		9/10th to 4.30 A.m. 1500 rounds being fired. The Enemys Artillery was fairly active shelling CHASSEUR CABARET FUZE Corner & DOUVE VALLEY. Several hostile Aeroplanes flew over our lines from 7-9.30 P.M. flying very high. Indirect Overhead fire as before was carried out. A Patrol from the Battalion in the line reported that they heard Enemies groans coming from the position to which our fire was directed the previous night at 9 P.m 2 small Balloons were seen passing over our lines going Westwards.	
	11th		Starts at Coy H.Qrs continued training in the line No 3 Section relieved No 3 Section in the line 8 O.R. Northants + 8 O.R. Sherwood Foresters arrived to be attached to the Coy for training the Carrying parties in action. Only intermittent shelling occured on the front. Indirect Overhead fire was carried out according to programme 600 rounds being fired	

Place	Date	Hour	Summary of Events and Information	Remarks and references to Appendices
LEINSTER RD NEUVE EGLISE T.28 B.15.75.	Sept 12th		8 O.R. Worcester Regt & 8 O.R. East Lancs reported for attachment to the Coy for training in carrying duties in action. Details at Coy HQrs filled all available Billets in the morning. At 12 P.M. the I.O. inspected the 32 O.R. attached from the Infantry Battalions of the Brigade & allotted them to their respective sections. At 3 P.M. the Inspector of Training for the II Army visited the Billets & mess & inspected the Cookhouse &c. He generally approved existing arrangements but recommended a larger variety of diet. Enemy Artillery & Aircraft were very active throughout the 24 hours. Our Indirect Overhead Fire provoked considerable retaliation.	
	13th		STRENGTH 10 Officers 208 Other Ranks 32 " " attached Details at Coy HQrs proceeded with ordinary training. Hostile Artillery heavily shelled ULTIMO AVENUE FLATTENED FARM & MESSINES RIDGE at 3 A.M & 8 P.M. Enemy Aeroplanes showed considerable activity throughout the day. At 10 A.M 2 E.A's flying over our lines & on being fired on returned air appearing to make a hurried descent. 2000 Rounds were fired on our Enemy work in front of Unclean Trench. 750 " " at Hostile Aircraft	

WAR DIARY
or
INTELLIGENCE SUMMARY

Army Form C. 2118.

Place	Date	Hour	Summary of Events and Information	Remarks and references to Appendices
LEINSTER RD NEUVE EGLISE T21 B.15.75	Sept. 14		The programme of training for details at Coy H.Qrs. was carried out. Hostile Artillery was generally more active on the front although by hostile Aircraft was not so active as usual. Our agent observers reported several fires behind the Enemy line - one very large one behind the SPINNING MILL. SAA supply of 80 Drill Rd Rounds & 60,000 rounds of SAA was sent up.	
	15th		Lieut SULLY returned from U.K. leave in the line from Sully relieving Lt Neale. No 3 Lieutenant relieved No 1 Section in the line. In accordance with a special programme and in conjunction with operations on our LEFT, indirect overhead fire was carried out from 1-15 Am to 4-15 Am. 11,000 rounds being fired at selected Targets.	
	16th		The programme was repeated again from 8.30 Pm 15th to 5 Am 16th. 12,000 rounds being fired. In addition 2800 rounds were fired at hostile Aircraft. 2nd Lieut Skinner & 2 other ranks returned from the Anti Aircraft Course at STEENWERCK. A voluntary Coy E. Service was held at the Billets for the Coy detail at 9.30 A.M. A hostile aeroplane was put down on our Front Line at 10.30 A.M.	

WAR DIARY or INTELLIGENCE SUMMARY

Army Form C. 2118.

Place	Date	Hour	Summary of Events and Information	Remarks and references to Appendices
REINSTER HK NRWIK EGI5K T2IB 15/5	Sept 16th Contd		In reply to our barrage at 10 A.M. lachrymatory shells & gas shells were fired into U.10.c & Corps line. Hostile Aircraft was active & notified at 5 p.m. 12000 rounds were fired by our Machine Guns at prearranged targets during the night 16/17th. In accordance with a request from the Division on our right Our M.G. at V11.A.1.8. was laid on an S.O.S. line on UNABLE TRENCH. At 6.30 A.M. a light went up breaking into 2 Reds 11 whites and owing to the lateness generally it was decided to open fire programme being carried out. There was again opened at 10 A.M. 1800 rounds being fired.	
	17th		The normal programme of harassing was carried out with attacks new details at Coy HQrs. A practice barrage was again sent down by our Artillery at 3 P.M. in conjunction with our M.G. fired a barrage on detailed positions firing 6225 rounds. Although this produced considerable retaliation from the Enemys Artillery he failed to find our positions, and it was only whilst our teams were returning after the programme was completed on to the	

WAR DIARY
or
INTELLIGENCE SUMMARY

Army Form C. 2118.

Place	Date	Hour	Summary of Events and Information	Remarks and references to Appendices
KEINSTEIN Sept			Original Battle positions were manned when No 40746 Pte J Gallagher was killed outright in the turret] The M.G. Pte Gallagher was banging at the time was badly damaged.	No 3428 Pte W Powell was wounded [wound extent in the turret]
NRUVE FOUCK F.F. T.21.B.15./6 North				
VICKERS LINES 18th			Coy lifted & moved to VICKERS LINES LE ROMARIN at 10 A.M. These huts were unoccupied immediately prior to being taken over by this Coy went in a very dirty & neglected condition & required a considerable amount of work to render them being habitable. A special programme of night firing was carried out in which only 3 M.G. were engaged. 9000 rounds being fired. A second practice barrage was put down at 6 A.M. until 6.42 A.M. when 13,750 rounds were fired. Several hostile Aeroplanes were engaged by M.G. fire & 1200 rounds were fired. Two men again observed in the direction of WARNETON. No 362252 Pte S Rice was slightly wounded No 1 Section relieved No 14 Section in the line.	
LE ROMARIN B 4 C 30.98.				
	19th		The tactical programme of night firing comprised 6 targets which were engaged by 4 M.G Guns 21,000 rounds were fired 800 rounds were also	

Army Form C. 2118.

WAR DIARY
or
INTELLIGENCE SUMMARY.
(Erase heading not required.)

Instructions regarding War Diaries and Intelligence
Summaries are contained in F. S. Regs., Part II.
and the Staff Manual respectively. Title pages
will be prepared in manuscript.

Place	Date	Hour	Summary of Events and Information	Remarks and references to Appendices
VICKERS LINES Sept LE ROMARIN 19th B.A.C.5099 Conta.	20th		Fired at hostile Aeroplanes	
		5.45 A.M.	At 5.45 A.M. in conjunction with operations to the North all M.M.G.s on barrage line opened fire on the WARNETON front & fired at the rate of 120 per minute at first steadying down to 60 rounds per minute until 6.20 A.M. firing 14,400 rounds. Our Gun position at SUGAR REFINERY was heavily shelled from 6-7 A.M. the tripod being completely destroyed. In spite of our heavy Artillery & M.G. barrage placed down on the German trenches no extraordinary lights were observed during the day or night.	
	21st		The details at Coy HQrs continued training and did considerable work in improving the Billets. In accordance with the Divisional Scheme new dispositions were made for our M.G. gun withdrawal from the Line. 5 emplacements were handed over to the 25th M.G. Coy and we took over one gun position from the 218th Coy taken up. Two oth. positions were abandoned. New gun positions were taken up. Hostile Artillery was only slightly active. ANTONS AVENUE & ULTIMO AVENUE being shelled during the night. At 5 P.M. the Enemy fired one shell towards PLOEGSTEERT WOOD which burst into a large number of lights.	

Army Form C. 2118.

WAR DIARY
or
INTELLIGENCE SUMMARY.

(Erase heading not required.)

Instructions regarding War Diaries and Intelligence Summaries are contained in F.S. Regs., Part II. and the Staff Manual respectively. Title pages will be prepared in manuscript.

Place	Date	Hour	Summary of Events and Information	Remarks and references to Appendices
MCKENZIE'S LINES LE ROMARIN BAC 50.98 contd	Sept 21		Hostile French Mortars sent shells into LA BASSE VILLE dropped at 11 P.M. A large number of parachute lights were observed to our left during the night all night lasted twice, a double light shew at 40° Mag from CANBERRA FARM for about 5 minutes. On two other occasions the Enemy fired Searchlights and A.A. Shells at it.	
	22nd		LA BASSE VILLE LA NUTTE PROWSE Point received attention from the Enemy's Artillery. Hostile M.G. fire fired down the DOUVE VALLEY and an Enemy Aeroplane dropped bombs on PLOEGSTEERT WOOD. A large number of men were observed along the Enemy's front. Training was carried on with details at Coy H.Qrs.	
	23rd		Details at Coy H.Qrs. went to Divisional Baths at 9 A.M. The Enemy's Artillery was fairly active throughout the day. Aeroplanes to & from 5 Crash this men caused by intermittent shelling. No. 102,672 L/Cpl Myers No. 103,716 Pte Campbell No. 102,883 Pte Davies No. 103,438 Pte Hohn No. 98,031 Pte Thompson being evacuated. No. 4 Section relieved teams from Nos 1 & 2 Sections	
	24th		The Enemy's Artillery was very active yesterday, the usual points being shelled. Training & Camp Improvements were proceeded with by details at H.Qrs	

(A7093) Wt. W12539/M1393 750,000. 1/17. D. D. & L., Ltd. Forms/C.2118/14.

WAR DIARY
or
INTELLIGENCE SUMMARY.
(Erase heading not required.)

Place	Date	Hour	Summary of Events and Information	Remarks and references to Appendices
VICKERS LINES LE ROMARIN B.A.C. 30.98.	Sept 24th contd.		Kent to Divisional Baths at 7.45 AM. Brigade Sports were held in the Afternoon. 2nd Brans went to A HQ at STEENWERCK to have the lantern slides scanned.	
	25th		The Hostile Artillery Armstrating prevailed on our front ST YVES AV. PROWSE POINT & CANTERAM FARM being sextra-heavily shelled. Warts at Coy HQ proceeded with training. Camp Improvements & protection of NCOs against Aircraft Bombs.	
	26th		Intermittent shelling of DOUVE VALLEY throughout the day by hostile Artillery. A few gas shells at times. No intelligence of information received special arrangements were made with Barrage Guns in case an enemy attack was made. Training was carried out procuctive by Coy HQno.	
	27th		Having found that our Gun Position taken over from 218th M Gun Coy had a very restricted field of fire owing to trees in its immediate vicinity the Gun Position was moved forward 100 yards to U.10.A.85.80. By request Indirect Overhead fire was carried out on to the neighbourhood of NICART FARM from 9 PM to midnight.	

WAR DIARY
or
INTELLIGENCE SUMMARY.

Army Form C. 2118.

Place	Date	Hour	Summary of Events and Information	Remarks and references to Appendices
VICKERS LINES LE ROMARIN. B.A.C. 50.98 cont.	Sept 27.		The neighbourhood of CANBERRA FARM was heavily shelled between 5-6 A.M. A number of Gas Shells were used. Hostile Aeroplane flew very low over the HQrs Billets about 10 P.m. M.G. fire was exchanged with it.	
	28th		A Battery relieved B Battery in the line. Sergt Skinner with 6 O.R. relieved the working party. Lieut Mitcham relieved Lieut Poole. Lt Sully relieved 2/Lt Skinner. Owing to the fact that 2/Lt Griffiths is undergoing medical treatment 2/Lt Smith's relief was postponed. DOUVE VALLEY was shelled 9 P.m - 2 A.m with Gas Shells. Hostile Long Range M.G. Fire was directed behind our SUBSIDIARY LINE.	
	29th		Reliefs at Coy HQrs proceeded with. Training Work on the improvement of trenches. There was the usual Hostile Artillery and Van Morrice in the activity of hostile Aircraft. Coy Strength 10 Officers. 99 O.R. 3 in hospt. 2 Lig Gourd Rocket Gunne. A hostile Aeroplane flying very low over the HQrs killed at 9 P.m 33 attacked 1 " was engaged by M.G. fire.	

Place	Date	Hour	Summary of Events and Information	Remarks and references to Appendices
VICKERS LINES LE ROMARIN B A C 50 98	Sept 30th		2/Lt Bruce, Cpl Stephenson + 10 OR proceeded to CAMIERS for M.G. School of G.H.Q. Small Arms School. Cpl Griffiths proceeded to the Divisional Gas School for 1 week Course. A working party of 1 NCO + 30 OR rank went to Brigade HQ at 9 AM as a working party. A Coy E served two Aids at 10.30 AM. Heavy barrage fire on all French lines at dawn DOUVE VALLEY + ROMSE R: being particularly shelled during the day. Aircraft was more active than usual. On occasions flights of 8-10 Enemy Aeroplanes crossed our lines repeated 1800 ten or more had transited the day at Mostel aeroplanes. 2 Enemy Aeroplanes were engaged when flying over Coy HQrs.	

24TH MACHINE GUN COMPANY

WAR DIARY

FOR the MONTH of OCTOBER 1917

By.
A.H.Weaver, 2Lt
for CAPT.
O.C. 24TH M.G. Coy.

Army Form C. 2118.

WAR DIARY
or
INTELLIGENCE SUMMARY.
(Erase heading not required.)

Instructions regarding War Diaries and Intelligence Summaries are contained in F. S. Regs., Part II. and the Staff Manual respectively. Title pages will be prepared in manuscript.

Place	Date 1919 Oct.	Hour	Summary of Events and Information	Remarks and references to Appendices
VICKERS LINES LARK CAMP & WARNETON SECTOR.	1st		2/Lt Griffiths attached to Artillery for 4 days from Gen¹ Hand Artillery Officer was attached to this Unit. The Hostile Artillery was less active on its front. Our Guns M.Gs carried out indirect fire on selected Targets behind the Enemy lines firing 3000 rounds. No 19401 L/Cpl Brooks 1/10/2/950 The Howards were sent to the Divisional Rest Camp at WIMEREUX.	
	2nd		Hostile Artillery considerably decreased. After shell burn SUBSIDIARY LINE AREA & REARWARD systems at 10 p.m. 13 A.M. the usual spasmodic shelling of the DOUVE VALLEY was more active than usual. Our M.Gs fired 3000 rounds on selected Targets. 2000 rounds were fired at Hostile Aeroplanes. B Battery relieved A Battery in the line.	
	3rd		The 20 mm emptied to establishment were returned to the Base by the 7.30 A.M. train from STEENWERCK. There was slight shelling of MEA FME at 5.20 – 5.30 Pm & h + 2 Am Shells were fired at MESSINES from a position NE of WARNETON. Hostile Aircraft were less active than usual. 3090 rounds were fired by M.Gs on selected Targets N.E. & Gas Shells dropped on ULTIMO AVENUE 10 – 10.30 Pm	

Army Form C. 2118.

WAR DIARY
or
INTELLIGENCE SUMMARY.
(Erase heading not required.)

Place	Date 1917	Hour	Summary of Events and Information	Remarks and references to Appendices
LARKS CAMP B & C 2.0 & WARNETON SECTOR	Oct 4th		The details with Coy HQrs moved from VICKERS LINES to LARKS CAMP. This latter was in a very tumble down condition & a great deal of work is necessary to make the place habitable. There was the usual shelling & Aircraft activity on the front.	
	5th		Details at Coy HQrs proceeded with training & work on the improvements of the Camp. The usual spasmodic shelling took place. Hostile Aircraft was considerably less active than usual. 350 rounds were fired by our MGs on Hostile Aeroplanes. L/Cpl Davis went to ABBEVILLE on a course of Horse Transport.	
	6th		Intermittent shelling of V.10 c. from 2-4 A.m. A few 5.9" on ULTIMO AVENUE, THATCHED COTT, RESERVE LINE & 8.30 p.m. Enemy has apparently only 3 groups of Artillery in this Sector. Enemy Aeroplanes were fairly active. At 9.51 P.m. a shock resembling that of a very large explosion was felt at V.15 c. The clock was put back 1 hour at midnight reverting to Greenwich Time.	
	7th		There was very little hostile shelling on our front during the day although hostile Aircraft was fairly busy. 200 rounds were fired by our MGs on Enemy Aeroplanes.	

WAR DIARY or INTELLIGENCE SUMMARY

Place	Date	Hour	Summary of Events and Information	Remarks and references to Appendices
LARKS CAMP B8.c.20 & WARNETON SECTOR	Oct 1917 8th		Capt A.M. PRATT the C.O. moved to A.N.H.Q. STEENWERCK to take over the duties of D.N.G.O. during the absence of Major MOOD. A Battery relieved R Battery in the Line. Hostile Artillery considerably decreased during the day also by aircraft. 2/Lt. G.B. STARKEY joined the Coy from the BASE.	
	9th		Hostile Artillery was more active during the day particularly in the neighbourhood of PROWSE POINT & DUCK BOARDS. A small Ammunition dump at PROWSE POINT was blown up by Hostile Shelling. Camp improvements were proceeded with. M.G. harassing fire was carried out from dusk to midnight on selected targets. 3000 rounds being fired.	
	10th		In accordance with the D.N.G.O's suggestion to new Gun positions were reconnoitred. Hostile Shelling slightly increased in Activity throughout the day. Persistent Shelling of DOUVE VALLEY & the EAST END of PLOEGSTEERT WOOD & PROWSE POINT, the latter being hit several times. Work was proceeded with at the Camp & some of the Huts were converted into a Recreation Room. M.G. harassing fire was carried out. 3000 rounds being fired.	

WAR DIARY
or
INTELLIGENCE SUMMARY.

Army Form C. 2118.

Place	Date	Hour	Summary of Events and Information	Remarks and references to Appendices
LARKS CAMP B8c20c9	1917 Oct 11		Pte Cockcroft reporting missing. Wires sent out on return Party which returned. The usual activity was displayed by the Enemy on RESERVE & SUPPORT LINES receiving much attention. Our aircraft was hotly engaged whenever Planes came within range of hostile AA Guns. Harassing fire with MGs was carried out on a hostile Battalion HQ & about 3000 rounds being fired provoking considerable retaliation. A fire was observed about 5.30 pm towards DEULEMONT.	
NAMETON SECTOR	12th		A further report has been received reporting Pte Cockcroft reported missing. It appears that he took refuge in a dug out at PROWSE POINT during some heavy shelling. He is believed to have been hit went to Dressing Station. PROWSE POINT & ANZAC A/Pn Coy A/Pn Coy at VISC. were heavily shelled. As soon as our MGs commenced their programme of Night firing Hostile Artillery heavily shelled the Gun positions but no casualties were caused. 3000 rounds were fired. Work on Camp improvements was carried out.	
	13th		The usual activity was displayed on the front	

Army Form C. 2118.

WAR DIARY
or
INTELLIGENCE SUMMARY.
(Erase heading not required.)

Instructions regarding War Diaries and Intelligence Summaries are contained in F. S. Regs., Part II and the Staff Manual respectively. Title pages will be prepared in manuscript.

Place	Date	Hour	Summary of Events and Information	Remarks and references to Appendices
LARKS CAMP B8.c.20 & WARNETON SECTOR	1917. Oct. 14th		B Battery relieved A Battery in the line. Increased activity prevailed throughout the day. Our forward area between FRONT & SUPPORT was heavily shelled at dusk in retaliation for our M.G. fire. M.G. harassing fire on the SPINNING MILL was carried out in the evening as considerable enemy movement had been observed here.	
	15th		Lieut H.G. FAULKNER from the 89th M.G. Coy arrived to-day & took up his appointment as 2nd in Command. Considerable hostile shelling took place & Adv Coy H.Qrs. was hit blowing in both entrances but causing no casualties. The FRONT & SUPPORT LINES were heavily shelled.	
	16th		There was less activity on the front than usual. The disposition of the M.Gs was changed in accordance with the DM 60. Plan and the new positions occupied by Midnight.	
	17th		One M.G. was hit by shell fire & the crosshead damaged. The SUPPORT LINE & ANTON'S AVENUE Adv Coy HQ & PROWSE POINT were all shelled during the day. Hostile Aeroplanes were very active. 1000 rounds were fired at them by our M.Gs.	
	18th		Increased activity in both hostile Artillery & Aircraft throughout the day. A few gas shells were sent over the SUBSIDIARY LINE & PROWSE POINT & MUD LANE. were shelled with 15 cm. Camp improvements were carried on.	

Army Form C. 2118.

WAR DIARY
or
INTELLIGENCE SUMMARY.
(Erase heading not required.)

Instructions regarding War Diaries and Intelligence Summaries are contained in F.S. Regs., Part II. and the Staff Manual respectively. Title pages will be prepared in manuscript.

Place	Date	Hour	Summary of Events and Information	Remarks and references to Appendices
LAAKS CAMP. B.&C. 20.	1917 Oct 19th		Reduced activity on the front. Work at Camp carried on in preparation for assisting in a RAID barrage positions were reconnoitred	
WARNETON SECTOR.	20th		Hostile Artillery Aircraft were fairly active throughout the day at the moral Areas were shelled	
	21st		A Raiding Party went over to the Enemys lines at 3.50 A.M. in conjunction with which M.G. put down a barrage on allotted areas for 35 minutes firing 6950 rounds. Cpl E. Swine Service was killed in the Bullet at 10 A.M. by Capt MAYNE C.F. of the Brigade Boxing contest 2 Cpl REES (the only entrant) was defeated on points. Hostile Artillery slightly decreased during the day except against our	
	22nd		Battery positions. Aerial activity greatly decreased. The details at Coy H.Q. attended the Baths at 4.30 P.M. Capt A.M. PRATT returned to duty as C.O. after acting as D.M. G.O. during the absence of Major MOOD	
	23rd		The football Match arranged with D Coy 1st WORCESTERS was cancelled	

Army Form C. 2118.

WAR DIARY
or
INTELLIGENCE SUMMARY.
(Erase heading not required.)

Instructions regarding War Diaries and Intelligence Summaries are contained in F. S. Regs., Part II. and the Staff Manual respectively. Title pages will be prepared in manuscript.

Place	Date	Hour	Summary of Events and Information	Remarks and references to Appendices
BARKS CAMP B.3.C.5.O. & WARRINGTON SECTOR	1917 Oct. 24th		Hostile Artillery & Aircraft slightly increased during the day particularly on the SUBSIDIARY LINE where one of the M.Gs was hit. As only the ingredients of the Traversing handles was hit the Gun continued in Action. Hostile Anti Aircraft Guns were particularly active against our Aeroplanes whenever they came within range of the Guns. L/Cpl Stocks, Pte Beardmore, Pte Brookes represented the Company in the Brigade Cross Country Run. L/Cpl Stocks finishing sixth. Pte Jones, Pte Jackson commenced a Course at the Divisional Lac School at 6 p.m.	
	25th		B Battery relieved A Battery in the Line. There was increased activity on the front	
	26th		L/Cpl Ball having previously attended an Anti Aircraft Course at BAILEUL has been reprimanded as an Instructor reported there for duty today Situation on the front was very quiet	
	27th		The drafts at Coy H.Qrs attended the Baths The following promotions were made 19630 A/Cpl Stephenson A. substantiated 3/8/17 vice L/Sgt Spooner promoted Sgt 19681 L/Cpl Collins promoted Cpl 16/9/17 vice L/Sgt Spooner appointed L/Sgt	

WAR DIARY
or
INTELLIGENCE SUMMARY.

Army Form C. 2118.

Place	Date	Hour	Summary of Events and Information	Remarks and references to Appendices
HRKS CAMP B.8. C.2.0. & WARNETON SECTOR.	1917 Oct 27th Cont.		72738 L/Cpl Thornton J Promoted Cpl 18/10/17 vice Cpl Ambrose to UK 19701 " Stokes F. Appointed A/Cpl 20/10/17 " Murray evacuated sick 19685 " Bonus.E " " " Pte/Cpl 29/9/17 vice L/Cpl Boden wounded 39007 " Pettitt.S " " " — 10/10/17 — Collins promoted Cpl 11036q " Smart.F. " " " — 10/10/17 — Thornton " Cpl Very quiet on the Front.	
	28th		Capt F Annis Service was killed in his Billet at 10 A.m by Capt MAYNE C.F. The transport attached this Battn at 5.30 P.m a Raiding Party was sent over to the Enemy Lines at 9 P.m in conjunction with which our M.G's put down a barrage on Elliot Area from 9p.m. to 9.35 P.m firing 14,100 rounds. Hostile Artillery was fairly active throughout the day in retaliation from hire cutting & put a Shell fairly fairly into a Shell hole L/Cpl Hopley Geo in bringing his Party out of action reported that he was badly James wounded in Head It is unofficially reported that he was also sprayed with Shrapnel on his way out to the Dressing Station Pte Bosworth was sent to the Dressing Station suffering from Shell Gas Poisoning	

Army Form C. 2118.

WAR DIARY
or
INTELLIGENCE SUMMARY.
(Erase heading not required.)

Instructions regarding War Diaries and Intelligence Summaries are contained in F. S. Regs., Part II. and the Staff Manual respectively. Title pages will be prepared in manuscript.

Place	Date	Hour	Summary of Events and Information	Remarks and references to Appendices
LARKS CAMP. B.8.c.2.0. 4	1917 Oct. 29th		On min-Relief took place, the 4 forward Coms being relieved by the 4 Coms in rear. Decreased Artillery on the Front. 1 Enemy Aeroplane flew low over SUPPORT LINE at 6 A.m.	
NAARNETON SECTOR.	30th		Slight Shelling of DOUVE VALLEY SUBSIDIARY RESERVE & SUPPORT LINES Hostile Aircraft fairly active	
	31st		Desultory Shelling of the SUBSIDIARY LINE & ULTIMO AVENUE Hostile Aircraft fairly active A Battery played the 25th Field Ambulance at football won 4 - 2 goals.	

WAR DIARY

of the

24th Machine Gun Company

by

Captain.A.M.PRATT

for the month of

NOVEMBER 1917.

1st December 1917.

A H Weaver Lt.
for O.C.
24th M.G. Company

Army Form C. 2118.

WAR DIARY
or
INTELLIGENCE SUMMARY.

(Erase heading not required.)

Instructions regarding War Diaries and Intelligence Summaries are contained in F. S. Regs., Part II. and the Staff Manual respectively. Title pages will be prepared in manuscript.

Place	Date	Hour	Summary of Events and Information	Remarks and references to Appendices
WARNETON SECTOR & LARKS CAMP B & C. 2.0.	Nov 1st		There was slight shelling of V11A1C & U10 during the day. A fire broke out at EAST END of ANTONS AVENUE in the early morning. Hostile M.Gs were fairly active. Our own M.Gs fired 1500 rounds at selected targets.	
	Nov 2nd		The day was very quiet with the exception of a few shells in U10 C. Our own M.Gs fired 1500 rounds on selected targets. A Rolling Reliefs of B. Battery in the line. Hostile Artillery was less active than normal.	
	3rd		Divine service was held for details at Coy H.Qrs. Details attended Baths at 2:30 P.M. Hostile Shelling was neg'ble except a few 10 cm shells on AROUSE POINT. Our M.Gs fired 1500 rounds on Dumps & Tracks.	
	4th		The situation was generally quiet. In the afternoon the 23rd M.G. Coy visited us & played football. The Coy gave a concert in the evening in the Recreation Room. Our M.Gs fired 1500 rounds on selected targets.	
	5th		An intercession with took place in the line. Increased hostile activity of Artillery & Aircraft throughout the day. Training was carried on in the morning. In the evening the Officers gave a Dinner to all Ranks out of the line who came out originally with the Division in November 1914.	
	6th			

WAR DIARY or INTELLIGENCE SUMMARY

Army Form C. 2118.

Place	Date	Hour	Summary of Events and Information	Remarks and references to Appendices
WARNETON SECTOR & LARK'S CAMP B 8 c 2.0	Nov 7th		Training was carried on in the morning. Slight hostile Artillery activity during the day. Sgt Williams J. went to CAMIERS on a months Course of Advanced Machine Gunnery.	
	8th		Training proceeded in the morning. Normal Activity on the front.	
	9th		Training continued in the morning. Fairly quiet on the front. A concert party "The Muddle Tops" from the 89th M.G. Coy. gave a much appreciated performance. Special Orders were issued for the No 2 s.M.G. to fire one gap in our front line in the event of certain signals being displayed. B Battery moved 7 Guns of the 25th M.G. Coy. 2nd Lt G.B Stanley came out of the line & went to Hospital. Normal activity on the front.	
	10th			
	11th		More activity than normal was displayed. HYDE PARK CORNER, SYKES AV. & MUD LANE being shelled.	
	12th		Normal activity on the front. 2 Officers of the 104th Australian M.G. Coy. & an O.R. per Gun Team went into the line to take over our Gun positions.	

Army Form C. 2118.

WAR DIARY
or
INTELLIGENCE SUMMARY.
(Erase heading not required.)

Instructions regarding War Diaries and Intelligence Summaries are contained in F. S. Regs., Part II. and the Staff Manual respectively. Title pages will be prepared in manuscript.

Place	Date	Hour	Summary of Events and Information	Remarks and references to Appendices
MARNETON EUROPA	Noon		The 19th Australian M.G. Coy. relieved the Coy. in the line. N.C.O. representatives	
LARKS CAMP B.8.0.2.0.	13th		went up with this Relief as Guides	
	14th		The day was spent in cleaning up Limno Limbers packing Limber Pulling Rollo x.c. Lt. Griffiths went in advance Billeting	
SHEET 36 F.24.C.	15th		The Coy. paraded at 8 A.m. moved to BLEU in the VIEUX BERQUIN AREA Arrived at destination 1.15 P.m. in good billets though scattered.	
	16th		The day was spent resting.	
	17th		Reveille at 3 A.m. Parade 5.30 A.m. Lt. Griffiths went in advance Billeting. One motor lorry was placed at our disposal.	
YPRES C.27.C.			The Coy. moved to CAESTRE by road entrained for YPRES detraining at YPRES at 12 noon the Company marched to St JEAN AREA in Support. The transport which came by road arrived in the same AREA at 6 P.m.	
	18th		Cpl. Pullick left for U.K. on a Special Course at GRANTHAM. The C.O. Lt. Faulkner Lt. Sully reconnoitred the forward AREA As a result of long range shelling Pte. Benton was wounded at 7.15 P.m.	

(A7092). Wt. W26350/M1993. 750,000. 1/17. D. D. & L., Ltd. Forms/C.2118/14.

Army Form C. 2118.

WAR DIARY
or
INTELLIGENCE SUMMARY.
(Erase heading not required.)

Place	Date	Hour	Summary of Events and Information	Remarks and references to Appendices
St JEAN C.27.c/6	Augt 19th		2/Lt Highland & 2/Lt Bruce reconnoitred the forward Area. 2 Casualties were caused by long range shelling. Pte Read & soldier R.E. Gunner.	
"	20.		The forward area was reconnoitred for a suitable barrage position. Instructions having been received for the Company to be withdrawn from the St JEAN AREA (from the Division) the Company moved off at 10 A.m into billets at the HOP FACTORY VLAMERTINGHE - BRANDHOEK ROAD	
HOP FACTORY BRANDHOEK H.8.A.50.95	21st		5 O.R. to Hospital mostly suffering from boils. A Lecture was given in the morning. Special T Bar frames were made for mounting Torpedos in huts & Soft Ground	
"	22nd		2 O.R. to Hospital. Inspection Parade in the morning	
"	23rd		2 O.R. to Hospital & 2/Lt Griffiths to Hospital. 2/Lt Skinner returned from Hospital. Lecture by CO on use of M.Go against hostile Attacks.	

(A7092). W1. W12859/M1293. 750,000. 1/17. D. D. & L., Ltd. Forms/C.2118/14.

Army Form C. 2118.

WAR DIARY
or
INTELLIGENCE SUMMARY.
(Erase heading not required.)

Place	Date	Hour	Summary of Events and Information	Remarks and references to Appendices
M.G. FACTORY, BRANDHOEK. A 8 A 50 & 85	Nov. 23rd Contd		In view of moving up into the line & support tomorrow the following Orders were issued. In order to provide relief for him in the fire teams will be made up to the strength of 2 N.C.O.s & 4 M Gunners re-attached Men to this purpose every available man now attached to M.Gs and Transport will be temporarily attached to the Gun Teams of Sections 2 & 3 re transfer to the fire will consist of 1 N.C.O. 2 Machine Gunners & 1 Marshall man. No 1 Section Gun on Team will be in reserve and will provide carrying parties & reinforcements if called upon. Promotions & Appointments. 10707 A/Cpl. Stocks ? to be substantiated vice Cpl Munday 106866 L/Cpl Garforth A to be A/Cpl vice Cpl Rothera to UK & posted to No 1 Section. 39242 L/Cpl Bonwill W to be paid L/Cpl vice L/Cpl Garforth. 11948 Pte Thomas appointed unpaid L/Cpl vice L/Cpl Fitzgerald to Hosp. 333326 - Pte Thornton appointed unpaid L/Cpl vice L/Cpl Garforth. Pte Morris H to take on duties of Postman temporarily. The Coy relieved the 21st M.G. Coy in the line on the night of 24/25th. In order to provide relief, Coy will consist of 6 O.R. divided into 2 Gun Teams. A 19 B	
PASSCHENDAELE Sector C 77 c 7.6	Nov 24			

Place	Date	Hour	Summary of Events and Information	Remarks and references to Appendices
PASSCHENDAELE SECTOR & C 27 c 7.6.	Nov 24th Contd		Inst teams A will take over Gun positions now occupied by the 215th M.G. Coy. Each team will take into the Line Gun, 1st Aid Case & Belt Boxes. Tripods & Belts will be taken over in the Line. A teams will parade at 11.30 A.m. in Route Order re Packs containing spare Rations Small kit Waterproof Sheet Haversacks Great Coats & Blankets will be handed into QM S Stores by 10.30 A.m. Relieving Teams under Lt Faulkner will proceed by motor Lorry at 12 noon to WIELTJE hence by road to WIELTJE where it will await arrival of the Company & then proceed with the Company at discretion of Lt Faulkner. On arrival of Lt Faulkner Guns & Limbers will leave at 10 A.m. to proceed to Adv Coy HQrs GRAVENSTAFEL where Guides from the 215th M G Coy will be waiting. 2 days & the uncooked portion of the days rations will be carried Cooked, Each team will also carry 1 Petrol Can of Water. Lt N Sully will be in command of Advance 1st Line Coy HQrs details & Transport will parade at 12.15 Noon prior to S. JEAN A Dump of non essential Stores will be formed in present QM Stores 1 NCO & 1 Man I/C All remain to guard this Dump	

Army Form C. 2118.

WAR DIARY
or
INTELLIGENCE SUMMARY.
(Erase heading not required.)

Place	Date	Hour	Summary of Events and Information	Remarks and references to Appendices
PASSCHENDAELE SECTOR & ST JEAN C.17.c.7.6	May 24th contd		The above relief was duly carried out. 2/Lt Skinner was wounded in the thigh & Pte Cockroft sprained his ankle. The dispositions of the Guns is as follows:- Reference sheet 28 NE & NW 1/20,000. A Group D.6.B.4.9. 2/Lt Skinner with teams 5A, 11BA to open fire on direct Targets. B Group V.30.c.5.5.2.5. 2/Lt Bruce teams 13A, 14A to open fire on direct Targets. C Group VENTURE FM under command of Infantry Commander supervision of 2/Lt BRUCE. 1st fire on direct Targets. D Group at MEETCHEELE under Lt Higham with teams 16A, 9A, 10A, 11A. 11BA to cover river on left. VENTURE FM to cover both sides of MEETCHEELE MOSSELMARKT ROAD. 7A & B Groups. Advanced Coy HQrs at GRAVENSTAFEL D.9.c.3.5. with OC 2nd M/C teams 7A & 11A in reserve.	
	May 25th		1 OR of details to Hospital. In accordance with COs instructions 32 Batt Boxes were sent up on Pack Animals this morning.	

(A7292) Wt. W.2858/M.1293. 750,000. 1/17. D.D. & L., Ltd. Forms/C.2118/4.

Army Form C. 2118.

WAR DIARY
or
INTELLIGENCE SUMMARY.

(Erase heading not required.)

Instructions regarding War Diaries and Intelligence Summaries are contained in F. S. Regs., Part II. and the Staff Manual respectively. Title pages will be prepared in manuscript.

Place	Date	Hour	Summary of Events and Information	Remarks and references to Appendices
PASSCHENDAELE East SECTOR & St JEAN. Contd. G.27.c.7.6.	25th		During night of 25/26. Our Gun dispositions were changed. 5 Guns of 92nd M.G. Coy. relieved our 5 at MEETCHEELE. GROUP D 1 " " 92nd " " " " Sunset VENTURE FM 2 Guides sent to WIELTJE DUGOUTS at 3 PM to guide 92nd M.G. Coy in. 1 of our Guns to relieve 1 Gun of 100th Coy at D6 B 78.24 to come under Group A. 2 of our Guns to relieve 2 Guns of 100th Coy at D6 B 91.03 & D6 A 88.15 to form GROUP E under Section Officer at D6 D 05.03. 2nd Lt Wright arrived from the Divisional School in place of 2nd Lt Wickes evacuated sick. As the Southall & Price of this concentration have been evacuated sick application has to-day been made for 2 OR to replace them. Cpl Collyns returned to duty from hospital. L/Cpl Pues " " " from ASC 1 OR complains of having attended from leave. The following Casualties have been caused in the Line. No 102985/3 Pte Hudson J. Whitehead A.} Killed 30296 6646 L/Cpl Eden S. 36110 Pte Harrison A. } Wounded 33326 " Christian } Wounded	

WAR DIARY
or
INTELLIGENCE SUMMARY.

Army Form C. 2118.

Place	Date	Hour	Summary of Events and Information	Remarks and references to Appendices
PASSCHENDAELE SECTOR. ST. JEAN. C27c76	Nov. 25th		At 7.15 P.m. the S.O.S. was sent up on our front. Our Artillery vigorously responded and the situation was pronounced Normal at 10 P.m. Lt SULLY relieved Lt. SAUNIER. 2 Coys under Lt. Col. Sellers & Lt Col Ryall returned to Rear H.Qrs having been relieved.	
	26th		Rations & Water were sent up at 8.15 A.M. Lpl Christison previously reported wounded has since died. Fresh instructions from AREA COMMANDANT BRANDHOEK Army acting on instructions from AREA COMMANDANT BRANDHOEK the Brigade the Transport Lines were moved to H.3.C.2.3.	
	27th		40,000 rounds of S.A.A. were sent up by Pack Animals at 2 A.M. 2 Lpls & 42 O.R. went up as a working party & those No 91131 Pte Edwards W. } were wounded. 19623 LCpl Maguire H 85041 Pte Leavy A 16387 Pte Candace A. 102872 Pte Mills J. 102872 Pte Mills J. Water was sent up by Pack Animals at 6 A.M.	

WAR DIARY or INTELLIGENCE SUMMARY

Army Form C. 2118.

Place	Date	Hour	Summary of Events and Information	Remarks and references to Appendices
PASSCHENDAELE SECTOR	Nov 28th		80 Bell Boxes were sent up the line at 1 A.M. Cpls & L/Cpls B.Rs went up as a working party at 2 A.M. Rations & full wire sent up at 6 A.M. 2/Lt Skinner previously reported wounded now reported died of wounds. Sgt Foot Griffin & Rozzel reported for duty from Hospital. Pte Baggot went to Hospital. Sick from the line.	
	29th		The C.S.M went up the line to take charge of Ammunition & Rations. 1 Sgt 1 Cpl & two O.Rs. went up as working party at 5 A.M. Col Griffiths returned from this party at 9 A.M. reported sick went down to Hospl. by M.O. of the Worcestershire Regt. together with 2 O.Rs. The C.S.M returned to Rear Coy HQrs at 4 P.M. Our Barrade was put on at 8 P.M. 14 attending. Pte Cox G. returned from the line at midnight ill. 2/Lt Smith returned from leave. A working party consisting of all those not in the Barrage Ration strength 27 in number went up as a working Party at 5 A.M.	
ST-JEAN C27C76	30th		Ration strength 27 in number. Rations & strafes for 3 days were sent up at 5-15 A.M.	

Army Form C. 2118.

WAR DIARY
or
INTELLIGENCE SUMMARY.

(Erase heading not required.)

Instructions regarding War Diaries and Intelligence Summaries are contained in F. S. Regs., Part II. and the Staff Manual respectively. Title pages will be prepared in manuscript.

Place	Date	Hour	Summary of Events and Information	Remarks and references to Appendices
PASSCHENDAELE SECTOR.	Nov 30th		At 2 P.M. 2/Lt Smith & the Barrage Battery went up to prepare the position returning at 3 A.M.	
St JEAN C.27.c.7.6.	Contd.		2 O.R. to Hospital. The following Casualties occured No 225789 Pte TOWNSHEND.R. 2nd Northants Killed No. 102994 - MORETON A. Wounded No 14931 " COSGROVE J. absent. He was sent from front to REAR H.Q. early in the morning thas not yet reported to Rear H.Q.	

WAR DIARY
of the
24th MACHINE GUN COMPANY.
for the
month of
DECEMBER 1917.
by

A Bennett.
Captain.

Commanding 24th Machine Gun Company.

Appendix A

24th Company, MACHINE GUN CORPS.

OPERATION ORDER.
by
Capt. A.M. PRATT.

1. During the operations the task of the Company will be:-
   (1) Barrage with 8 Guns.
   (2) Support Infantry with 7 Guns.

2. Lieut SULLY will barrage with 8 Guns from D.5.d.70.20.

3. Defence Guns as below, will move forward so as to reach positions by dawn on ZERO day.
   "B" Group (2/Lt BRUCE) will move Guns to about V.30.b.9.4.
   V.30.b.5.8.
   "A" Group (2/Lt SMITH) will move Guns to about D.6.b.9.7.
   W.25.c.9.7.
   W.25.c.0.9.

   "E" Group (Lieut HIGHAM) One Gun will remain in present position.
   One gun will move to D.6.b.40.95. to replace "A" Group.

4. For purpose of moving teams of defence guns will be reonforced by
   1 N.C.O.
   2 O.R.   at dusk 1st December.
   ("E" Group will not be reinforced).

5. Teams moving will carry:-
   Gun.
   Tripod
   1st Aid Case.
   8 Belt Boxes.
   2 Shovels.

6. As soon as guns are in position reports will be sent to report centre.

7. Report Centre will be at The GRAF D.5.d.5.6.

8. ZERO hour will be notified later.

1/12/17.   O.C. 24th Machine Gun Company.

Copies to:- 1.
             2.
             3.
             4.

APPENDIX B

24th Company, MACHINE GUN CORPS.

Appendix to OPERATION ORDERS
by
Captain. A.M. PRATT.

Ref Map. SHEET. 28.N.E. & 20.S.E. 1/20000.

FIRE CONTROL ORDERS
BARRA for
BARRAGE BATTERY of 8 M.Guns. numbered from Right to Left

Reference Object. PASSCHENDAELE CHURCH.

TASK "A"   1, 2 & 3 Guns. (on Target (1).)
        Direction.   12° LEFT.
        Elevation.   6° 57' to 8° 57' search.
        60 rounds per minute.

        4, 5 & 6 Guns. (on Target (2).)
        Direction.   15° LEFT.
        Elevation.   5° 33' to 6° 57' search.
        60 rounds per minute.

        7 & 8 Guns. (on Target (3).)
        Direction.   15° LEFT.
        Elevation.   8° 9' to 10° 4' search.
        60 rounds per minute.

TASK "B".   (on Target (4).)
        Direction.   18° LEFT.
        Elevation.   4 Right Guns. 5° 6' to 10° search.
                       4 Left Guns. 10° to 5° 6' search.
        60 rounds per minute.

TASK "C"   (on Target (5).)
        Direction.   22° LEFT.
        Elevation.   4 Right Guns. 5° 45' to 10° search.
                       4 Left Guns. 10° to 5° 45' search.
        60 rounds per minute.

APPENDIX C

FIRE ORDERS.

TIME.	0+25° to 0+28°	0+31° to 0+34°	0+37° to 0+40°	0+55° to 0+58°	0+1-1° to 0+1-4°	0+1-7° to 0+1-10°	0+1-25° to 0+1-28°	0+1-31° to 0+1-34°
TASK.	B.	C.	A.	C.	D.	A.	A.	D.
Direction.	12° left 15° left	25° left	12° left	22° left	18° left	12° left 15° left	12° left, 15° left	15° left.

TIME	0+1-37° to 0+1-40°	0+1-55° to 0+1-58°	0+3-1° to 0+3-4°	0+3-7° to 0+3-10°	0+3-25° to 0+3-28°	0+3-31° to 0+3-34°	0+3-37° to 0+3-40°	0+3-55° to 0+3-58°
TASK.	C.	D.	C. E.	D. A.	A. A.	A. A.	D. E. C.	B.
Direction.	22° left	18° left	25° left 15° left	12° left 15° left.	18° left	12° left	22° left	18° left

TIME	0+3-1° to 0+3-4°	0+3-7° to 0+3-10°	0+3-25° to 0+3-28°	0+3-31° to 0+3-34°	0+3-37° to 0+3-40°	0+3-55° to 0+3-58°	0+4-1° to 0+4-4°	0+4-7° to 0+4-10°
TASK.	C.	A.	A.	D.	C.	D.	C.	A.
Direction	22° left 15° left	12° left 15° left	12° left 18	25° left 18	22° left	25° left 18	22° left	12° left 15° left.

TIME	0+4-25° to 0+4-28°	0+4-31° to 0+4-34°	0+4-37° to 0+4-40°	0+4-55° to 0+4-58°	0+5-1° to 0+5-4°	0+5-7° to 0+5-10°	0+5-25° to 0+5-28°	0+5-31° to 0+5-34°
TASK.	A.	D.	C.	D.	E.	A.	A.	B.
Direction.	12° left 15° left	18° left	22° left	18° left	22° left	12° left 15° left	12° left 15° left	18° left

TIME.	0+5-37° to 0+5-40°	0+5-55° to 0+5-58°	0+6-1° to 0+6-4°	0+6-7° to 0+6-10°
TASK	C.	B.	C.	A.
Direction	22° left	18° left 15° left	12° left 15° left	12° left

TIME of FIRING.   APPENDIX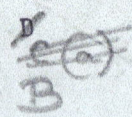
                                                 B

TASK "A"   0 + 37 min. - 0 + 40 min.   0 + 1 hr 7 min. - 0 + 1 hr 10 min
           0 + 1 hr 25 min - 0 + 1 hr 28 min.
           0 + 2 hr 7 min. - 0 + 2 hr 10 min.
           0 + 2 hr 25 min. - 0 + 2 hr 28 min.
           0 + 3 hr 7 min. - 0 + 3 hr 10 min.
           0 + 3 hr 25 min. - 0 + 3 hr 28 min.
           0 + 4 hr 7 min. - 0 + 4 hr 10 min.
           0 + 4 hr 25 min. - 0 + 4 hr 28 min.
           0 + 5 hr 7 min. - 0 + 5 hr 10 min.
           0 + 5 hr 25 min. - 0 + 5 hr 28 min.
           0 + 6 hr 7 min. - 0 + 6 hr 10 min.

TASK "B"   0 + 25 min. - 0 + 28 min.
           0 + 1 hr 1 min. - 0 + 1 hr 4 min.
           0 + 1 hr 31 min. - 0 + 1 hr 34 min.
           0 + 1 hr 55 min. - 0 + 1 hr 58 min.
           0 + 2 hr 31 min. - 0 + 2 hr 34 min.
           0 + 2 hr 55 min. - 0 + 2 hr 58 min.
           0 + 3 hr 31 min. - 0 + 3 hr 34 min.
           0 + 3 hr 55 min. - 0 + 3 hr 58 min.
           0 + 4 hr 31 min. - 0 + 4 hr 34 min.
           0 + 4 hr 55 min. - 0 + 4 hr 58 min.
           0 + 5 hr 31 min. - 0 + 5 hr 34 min.
           0 + 5 hr 55 min. - 0 + 5 hr 58 min.

TASK "C"   0 + 31 min. - 0 + 34 min.
           0 + 55 min. - 0 + 58 min.
           0 + 1 hr 37 min. - 0 + 1 hr 40 min.
           0 + 2 hr 1 min. - 0 + 2 hr 4 min.
           0 + 2 hr 37 min. - 0 + 2 hr 40 min.
           0 + 3 hr 1 min. - 0 + 3 hr 4 min.
           0 + 3 hr 37 min. - 0 + 3 hr 40 min.
           0 + 4 hr 1 min. - 0 + 4 hr 4 min.
           0 + 4 hr 37 min. - 0 + 4 hr 40 min.
           0 + 5 hr 1 min. - 0 + 5 hr 4 min.
           0 + 5 hr 37 min. - 0 + 5 hr 40 min.
           0 + 6 hr 1 min. - 0 + 6 hr 4 min.

APPENDIX "D".   PROGRAMME OF COMPANY TRAINING.

Dec. 5th.   Lectures by C.O. The Compass, Maps, Finding position on Maps
                         Degrees, The Traversing Dial.
               Mechanism under Section Sgts, Elementary Gun Drill.

Dec. 6th   Lectures by C.O. Zero Lines, Aiming Posts.
               Stoppages, Elementary Gun Drill. Anti-Aircraft Practice.

Dec. 7th.   Lectures by C.O. Gas Warfare. Barrage Fire.
               Inspection of Anti-gas Appliances. Anti-gas Drill.
               Aiming with Gas Masks on. T.O.E.T.

Dec. 8th.   CHURCH PARADES. Lectures by C.O. The Elevating Dials. Lifting
               T.O.E.T. Anti-Aircraft Practice. Mechanism.

Dec. 9th.   CHURCH PARADES

Dec. 10th.   Lecture by C.O. Night Firing.
               T.O.E.T. T.O.E.T with Gas Masks. Belt Filling.

Dec. 11th.   Short Route March in full marching oredr.
               Revolver practice. Anti-Aircraft practice.

Dec. 12th.   Battery Drill by Sections.
               Constructions of Emplacements and Shelters.

Dec. 13th.   Battery Drill by Sections. Anti-Aircraft Drill
               Stripping and Repairs. Mechanism and Stoppages.

Dec. 14th.   Lecture by C.O. Duties of M.G's in Trench Warfare.
               Practice with Range Cards. Battery Drill

Dec. 15th.   Kit Inspection. Inspection of Gun Kit.
               Stripping and Repairs. Revolver Practice.

Dec. 16th.   CHURCH PARADES.

Dec. 17th.   Gas Drill. T.O.E.T. ½ Hr Lecture by Section Officers.
               "Indirect Fire" Lecture by C.S.M. to all Cpls and Lcpls
               "Discipline".

Dec. 18th.   Inspection by G.O.C. 24th Infantry Brigade.

Dec. 19th.   No.1.Section on range firing, Table "C" Part.1.
               No.2, 3 & 4 Sections, Gas Drill, Gun Drill.
               Lecture by Section Officers "Indirect Fire". Refilling Belts

Dec. 20th.   No.2.Section on range firing, Table "C" Part.1.
               No's 1, 3 & 4 Sections Gas Drill, Gun Drill, Mechanism.
               Lecture by Section Officers "BARRAGE" Refilling Belts.

Dec. 21st.   No's 3 & 4 Sections firing on range, Table "C" Part.1.
               No's 1 & 2 Sections, Barrage Drill.
               Lecture by Battery Officer. "Use of Clinometer & Spirit Leve

Dec. 22nd.   No Parades. Christmas Festivities.

Dec. 23rd.   CHURCH PARADES.

War Diary Dec 1917.
APPENDIX E.

24th MACHINE GUN COMPANY.

Narrative of the Operations on 1st/2nd December 2D2V1917.

For the Operations the task of the Company was
   (1) Barrage with 8 Guns
   (2) Support the Iffantry with 7 Guns

Lieut SULLY was ordered to conduct the Barrage.
The position for this was at D.5.d.70.20., having been previously reconnoitred by the C.C. This choice of position seems to have been justified as no casualties were incurred by this Battery.
Regarding (2), the following arrangements were made:-
The Groups as below were ordered to move forward so as to reach positions by dawn on Zero Day.
   (1) A Group under 2nd Liuut SMITH to about D.6.b.9.7., W.25.c.0.9., and W.25.c.0.9.
   (2) B Group under 2nd Lieut BRUCE to about V.30.b.9.4.and V.30.b.5.8.
   (3) B Group under Lieut HIGHAM; one gun to remain in original position and one gun to move to D.6.b.40.95., to replace A Group.

For the purposes of moving, teams of Defence Guns were reinforced by 1 N.C.O.and 2 O.R. at Dusk on the 1st December.

Report Centre was fixed at the GRAF, D.5.d.5.6.

DECEMBER 2nd.
Zero Hour was fixed at 1.55 a.m. 2/12/17.

The Barrage as in (1) above opened at Zero plus 25 minutes and was carried out according to schedule attached (Appendices E &F), firing being carried on intermittently until Zero plus 6 hours 10minutes, and being repeated in the afternoon from 3.25.p.m. until 6.10.p.m.
As time permitted adequate arrangements' being made beforehand, no difficulty was experienced with regard to Ammunition Supply or Belt Filling. Owing to the very indifferent quality of Ammunition available, ("J"), an undue proportion of stoppages occured, (mostly nos 1 & 4).
A hostile aeroplane flew very low over the Barrage Position from 3.15. to 3.45.p.m., dropping green lights, but was eventually driven off by no 5 Gun, which was detailed solely for Anti-Aircraft Work. No apparent action followed.

Respecting the Defence Guns:-
   (1) 2nd Lieut SMITH moved forward with his three Guns at the appointed time, and reached the selected position. Here, however, he suffered very severe casualties as far as two guns were concerned, he himself being badly wounded. All his N.C.O's were either killed or wounded, and only one man was left to man each gun. All this damage was caused by Machine Gun Fire. It appears that one of the survivors brought back the two guns to Lieut HIGHAM soon after. Corpl THORNTON with the remaining Gun got into position at the selected place without suffering casualties, and remained there with a good field of fire until relieved the same evening.
   (2) 2nd Lieut BRUCE found the position at V.30.b.9.4. in the hands of the enemy, the Gun was therefore placed 100 yds short of it. The other Gun got into position at V.30.b.5.8. 2nd Lieut BRUCE fell into a well whilst endeavouring to get into touch with the Group on his Right, and was eventually admitted to Hospital suffering from Debility.
   (3) Lieut HIGHAM moved forward as ordered to D.G.b.40.95.

Victor Sully Lieut.
O.C. 24 M.G.Coy

Appendix "F"

24th Company, MACHINE GUN CORPS.

RELIEF ORDERS by Captain. A. BENNETT.
for 27th December 1917.

Reference Map. Sheet. 28. N.E. 1/20000.

The Company will relieve the 224th M. G. Company in the line on the morning of the 27th inst.

Distribution. Barrage Group. At approximately
"A" Battery ... D.4.b.40.55.
"B" Battery ... D.4.b.26.30.,
consisting of
4 Guns of No.3. Section) Composing "A" Battery under
2 Guns of No.1. Section) Lieut. C. LEAVER.

4 Guns of No.4. Section) under 2nd Lt. R. C. SCOTT) Composing
4 Guns of No.2. Section) under Sgt Skinner.   ) "B" Battery.

Back Area Guns. One Gun No.1. Section at WURST FARM D.7.d.75.96. and 2 Guns attached from 23rd M. G. Company at KORES, D.9.c.65.65. under 2nd Lt. G. St C. MURRAY.

Teams. Each team will consist of 4. O.R. A N.C.O. or paid Lcpl will be with each Sub-section.

Parades, etc. Reveille.   3. a.m.
            Breakfast.   3-30.a.m.
Lieut. LEAVER with "A" Battery will move off at   4-30.a.m.
2nd Lt. SCOTT with No.4. Section will move off at 4-45.a.m.
Sgt Skinner with No.2. Section will move off at   5. a.m.
(plus Advd Company Hd Qrs, consisting Ptes Chiswell & Roberts, 1 Runner from each Section and C.O's Batman).
2nd Lt. MURRAY with back area Guns will move off at 5-15.a.m.

Dress:- Fighting Order plus Great-coats and Jerkins.
2 Days rations will be carried.
Tripods and Belt Boxes will be taken over from 224th Company
No's 1 of teams will personally see their Guns loaded on Pack Animals, ½ hr before moving off in each case.

Each group on moving off will proceed to WATERLOO. D.9.d.9.8. where guides from 224th Company will be met.

Officers will ensure that all Battle Maps, details of Target Lines of Fire, Elevations, etc are taken over before relieved Officers leave their positions.

Officers will report relief complete in person to O.C. Company at Advd Company Hd Qrs LAAMKEEK D.10.b.60.25.

Rations. 2 days rations will be carried on the man. Rations will be sent up every two days by pack animals. 14 tins of water will be despatched daily. All to leave St JEAN, X Rds C.27.d.30.25. arriving at WATERLOO at 7-30.a.m.

All meat will be cooked at Rear Company Hd Qrs.

Rations for Teams of 23rd Company will be sent up by 24th Company. 23rd Company will send rations for 9 men to reach Rear Hd Qrs 24th Company by 5.p.m. daily.

14 tins of water will be at Transport by 5.p.m. to-night 26th inst.

Handing over.

(2).

Handing over. 15 Tripods and 160 Belt Boxes have been handed over to
                234th Company.

Communication. Communication to Rear Hd Qrs will be maintained through
               Hd Qrs Support Battalion, BELLE VUE. D.4.d.7.2.

                                                       Victor Lucy Lieut.

26/12/17   for C.O. 34TH Machine Gun Company

                       Copies to:- 1. 23rd M. G. Company.
                                   2. 234th M. G. Company.
                                   3. O.C. Company.
                                   4. Transport Officer.
                                   5. Lieut. LEAVER
                                   6. 2nd Lt. SCOTT.
                                   7. 2nd Lt. MURRAY.

WAR DIARY or INTELLIGENCE SUMMARY

Army Form C. 2118.

Reference Map: Sheet 28 N.W. 1/20,000, Sheet 28 N.E. 1/20,000, BASE 1/40,000

Place	Date	Hour	Summary of Events and Information	Remarks and references to Appendices
D.S.D 76/70 (Sheet 28 NE)	31/10/17	—	The Barrage Group (8 guns under Lt A.V. SULLY) assembled at position of B.M.	See Appendix A. WH.
PASCHENDAELE	1/11/17	1.55 AM	ZERO hour. The barrage guns fired on per Appendix B. The close defence guns manned as per Appendix C. Canadian's service action — 1/Lt C.P. SMITH, 1/Lt E.T. BRUCE, 1/4 D.R. [?], 2 O.R. Killed. Capt A.M. PRATT – Gassed.	WH Appendix B. WH Appendix C. WH.
	1/11/17	6.30 pm	Barrage Group withdrew and returned to camp at WIELTJE	WH
		8 pm	Close defence guns released by Genl. O.C. 18th C. Div. Returned to camp at WIELTJE	WH
WIELTJE	2/11/17	1.30 pm	Coy from parade at 1.30 pm. Men entrained.	WH
		8 pm	Detrained at WIZERNES and marched to VAL-D'ACQUIN where Company was billeted.	WH
		11 pm	Transport arrived VAL-D'ACQUIN at 11.15 pm.	WH
VAL-D'ACQUIN	3/11/17		Capt PRATT admitted to hospital — gassed. Lt H.S. FAULKNER O.C. (2/L). Armament commanded. Company inspected in clearing equipment, baths and refitting.	WH
	4/11/17		Company engaged in training (Appendix D)	WH & Appx D
	5/11/17		Company training (Appendix D)	WH
	6/11/17		Company training (Appendix D)	WH
	7/11/17		Company training (Appendix D)	WH
—	8/11/17		[?] Ref [?] 15 O.R. Church Parade	WH

WAR DIARY or INTELLIGENCE SUMMARY

Army Form C. 2118.

Place	Date	Hour	Summary of Events and Information	Remarks and references to Appendices
VAL DI-ACQUIN	10th	—	Company training. Transport inspected by G.O.C. 24th Inf Bde.	
— do —	11th	—	Company transport inspected by A.D.V.S. Officer A. BENNETT & Company had received command. Six other Officers & C. LEAGUE joined Company. 2/Lt RE SCOTT reported. Also 17 O.R.s	
— do —	12th	—	2/Lt A. H. WEAVER proceeded on leave to U.K.	
— do —	13th	—	Company training (Appendix D). Inspection of Anti Gas appliances by Bde.	
— do —	14th	—	Gas Office. Company training. Officers attended lectures at VISQUES on R.E. Work and Aerial Photography and at BOIS BINGHEM on Musketry.	
— do —	15th	—	Company training (Appendix D) Church Parade	
— do —	16th	—	— do —	
— do —	17th	—	— do —	
— do —	18th	—	O.C. 24th Inf Bde inspected Company including transport at VAL-D'-ACQUIN. at 11 am. 17 O.R. reinforcements arrived.	
— do —	19th	—	Company training. No. 1 Section Army Workshop. O.C. 2nd Army Inspected transport. Capt. F.C. HIGHAM to Camouflage School BOULOGNE.	

WAR DIARY or INTELLIGENCE SUMMARY

Army Form C. 2118.

Place	Date	Hour	Summary of Events and Information	Remarks and references to Appendices
VAL-D-LAMBRES	23rd	—	Company formed. 2nd Lieuts Army (Appendix D) & 2nd Lt G.S.C. MURRAY joined from CAMIERS. 2nd Lt FAULKNER proceeded to take command of 196 M.G. Coy. 2nd Lt. SULLY took over duties of 2nd i/c in command of company.	
–do–	24th	—	2nd Lieuts Army, Tibbs and Murray to AA Course, LOUIE AERODROME. 2nd Lt STARKEY to Bombing train. (Appendix D)	
–do–	25th	—	Gas training continued. No Parade.	
–do–	23rd	—	Gas training continued. Lectures by Liaison Officers.	
–do–	24th	—	Company transport moved with a view to staging at WORMECAPPELLE for the night 24/25 Dec. Company employed on gas and reserve training. Captain HIGHAM took over duties of transport officer in from Lt DEANS (ordinary)(going to UK)	24TB Orders 226
	25th	5 am	Company 5 and Company moved off at 6.40 am via ACQUIN, VAL de LUMBRES, ESETQUES to WIZERNES, where entrained at 10.30 am.	
		10.30am	addressed by the G.O.C. VIII Corps, Lt. Gen. Sir AYLMER HUNTER-WESTON. Detrainment at St JEAN. Coy arrived in quarters under convoy in Rue	
St JEAN (YPRES)		3.15pm	JUNCTION ANNEXE CAMP, St JEAN at 3.15 pm. Transport arrived in Rue not far camp at 4.30 pm. O.C. Coy visited HQ of 224 L.M.G. Coy (14th Division) in the line to arrange details of relief. Guns and personnel for the Line took down on rovelment	
	26th		of transport lines and quarters of personnel	
BARRAQUE POS'NS W; of CORPSE (NN of PASSCHENDAELE)	27th	3am	Reveillé 3am. Company moved off at intervals from 4.30 to 5.15 am. to	

Army Form C. 2118.

WAR DIARY
or
INTELLIGENCE SUMMARY.
(Erase heading not required.)

Instructions regarding War Diaries and Intelligence Summaries are contained in F. S. Regs., Part II. and the Staff Manual respectively. Title pages will be prepared in manuscript.

Place	Date	Hour	Summary of Events and Information	Remarks and references to Appendices
BARRACK POSN= WOLF COPSE (NW of PASSCHENDAELE)	28th Dec	Dawn	Relieved 224th M.G. Coy in Barrage Positions at WOLF COPSE NW of PASSCHENDAELE and in Back Area Defence Positions on ABRAHAM HEIGHTS. Company HQ at LAMKEEK. Lt LEAVER commanded Barrage Group (4 guns) assisted by 2/Lt SCOTT. 2/Lt MURRAY manned Back Area positions with 1 gun of No1 Section and 2 guns attached from 23rd M.G. Coy. Lt SOUY was i/c details at Junction Annex. 1 gun of No 1 Section was mounted for AA work at ST JEAN. Work on AA defences Transport Lines and AA defences carried quietly in the Rine. No casualties.	Appendix F
	28th		Work at Road HQ. ST JEAN on revetment of shelters and Transport Lines & ok on position and ammunition stores in the Rine. No casualties. Enemy shelled encampments at ST JEAN with approximately 100 15 cm howitzer shells. The point was temporarily cleared. 2/Lt WEAVER rejoined.	
	29th		Quiet in the Rine again. Work as on 28th	
	30th		Work at Road HQ on new M.G. Quarter in YPRES under D.M.G.O. Quiet in the Rine.	
	31st	6.15am	day out no casualties. Enemy raid on Line at Cliff 615 am. Readying in 1 SOS rocket's being fired on Centenary Point at 6.20. Barrage Battery opened fire at 6.25am and had 6000 rounds with 6.30. Our Company was relieved by 25th M.G. Coy. relief being completed by 8am 24, TB 20r was wounded when guiding in relieving team to Back Area gun positions On relief, teams moved by Covd from WIETJE and details and transport by hand route to Reserve Billets BRANDHOEK. Billets and Transport Lines very good.	Order 227

(A7092) Wt. W12859/M1293. 750,000. 1/17. D. D. & L., Ltd. Forms/C.2118/14.

WAR DIARY
INTELLIGENCE SUMMARY.

Army Form C. 2118.

11th Machine Gun Company

Place	Date	Hour	Summary of Events and Information	Remarks and references to Appendices
Sheet 27 1/40000	1.2.1918		The Coy carried out training in accordance with training programme.	
		2.30pm	A First Football match was played at 2.30 p.m. The 2nd in Command went to Cassier to see demonstration Garage.	
	2.2.18	11AM	Church parade under Capt. Bennett. In afternoon the Officers of Batt. played the Sergeants. Result 2-nil in favour of Sergeants.	
	3rd Feb.		Two Sections carried out firing practice on the range the remainder of Coy carried on the usual programme of training.	
	4th Feb.		The Coy carried out usual programme of training. No 16369 Cpl Sheathatwarded Belgian Croix de Guerre. Divisional Routine order N° 3218 Special orders issued by Batt. showing ceremonial parade for Guard Mounting and Batt. inspection by a General Officer.	
	5th Feb.		The Coy fired range practices, stoppages. Special classes such as Signalling Rangefinding carried out usual programme. A lecture was given by C.O. on Barrage Fire.	
	6th Feb.		Coy carried out usual programme of training. Special classes as usual. In accordance with the new organisation shortly to be issued by G.H.Q. the personnel of 218th Coy was transferred to 23, 24 + 25th Coys. One complete Section to each Coy. Capt Jones temporarily appointed in Command of Coy, Capt Higham temporarily 2nd in Command of 23rd Coy, Capt. Bennett on leave in U.K.	

Army Form C. 2118.

WAR DIARY
or
INTELLIGENCE SUMMARY.
(Erase heading not required.)

Instructions regarding War Diaries and Intelligence Summaries are contained in F.S. Regs., Part II. and the Staff Manual respectively. Title pages will be prepared in manuscript.

Place	Date	Hour	Summary of Events and Information	Remarks and references to Appendices
Sheet 27 1/40000	Feb 7th 1918		The Battalion paraded for inspection by C.O. at 10 a.m. in full Marching Order.	
	Feb 8th		Coy. carried out usual programme of training in Camp. Fourth Army referring to Gas Projector Attacks by enemy was read out on parade.	
		2 p.m.	The Coy. paraded for baths. The Battalion football team won the Div. final.	
	Feb 9th		Orders for move issued today. The usual programme of training was carried out.	
	Feb 10th		Major Angel arrived 2nd i/c Battalion. 2nd Lt. Murray and party went in advance as a Billeting party. Limbers were packed ready for move tomorrow.	
	Feb 11th		The Battn. paraded at 6 A.M. and marched to Gouzeaucourt entraining there. The Coy. detrained near Yprès and marched to Vlamertinge to Tilleuls. Arrangements were made to relieve the 229th M.G. Coy. 29th Div. the following day. Transport proceeded by road.	

Operation Orders by
                    Capt Tonks O.C. 'B' Coy

'B' Coy will take over

1. Gun positions in the support area from the 227th M.G. Coy. Coy H.Qrs. will be at GALLIPOLI D 13 d 42

2. One full N.C.O & one junior N.C.O. and 6 other ranks will man each pair of guns.

3. Lt. Leaver will take 1 Signaller with him. 2nd Lt Hardy will take 1 Signaller with him. Adv. Coy H.Qrs will have
    2 Signallers
    2 Runners
The C.S.M. will detail these men to join respective sections. He will be at advanced Coy H.Qrs.

4. 10 filled belt boxes per gun will be handed over and remaining four per gun taken in by teams. All remaining gun kit will be taken in by gun teams.

5. Range Cards, Sentries, information boards and sentries order boards will be prepared for each gun position.

6. Guns Nº 17, 18, 19 & 20 will be mounted for A.A. work by day. Mountings will be taken over from 227 Coy

7. In every case the Section Officer will live with one pair of Guns and the Section Sergt. with the other pair of the Section.

8. It must be impressed on all ranks that any movement by day in the foward area will inevitably draw shell fire.

9. The S.O.S. Signal is
    RED
    over
    GREEN
    over
    YELLOW.

All Guns will have S.O.S lines with aiming posts out & will normally be laid on these lines.

10. Each Section is responsible for making itself acquainted with position of Coy Hd Qrs.

11. Sections will report by Runner 'relief complete' to Adv. Coy Hd Qrs.

12. The exact map reference of each Gun position will be reported to Coy Hd Qrs. at earliest opportunity.

13. Coy details will be at WIELTJE C 27 d 58 (Sheet 27.)

           Capt. Tonks
           O.C. 'B' Coy
           8th Divnl. M.G. Battn.

11.2.18.

Ref. Para. 3.
    No 8 Section will take over 17, 18, 19, & 20 Gun positions & No 10 Section will take over 21, 22, 23, & 24.
No 6 & 7 Sections will be at advanced Coy Hd Qurs.

           O.C. 'B' Coy.

Army Form C. 2118.

WAR DIARY
or
INTELLIGENCE SUMMARY.
(Erase heading not required.)

Place	Date	Hour	Summary of Events and Information	Remarks and references to Appendices
28 N.E.1 1/10,000	12th Sept 1918		The Coy paraded at 8.30 a.m. and marched to Ypres where the men washed and rubbed their feet. At 1.30 p.m. the Coy moved up the line. Guides were met at the Somme Dressing Station Map reference (D13.C.4) The Coy took over 10 Coll-lores for guns from the 227th Coy. (See Attached operation orders) Details and a 2nd in Command remained in Camp in WILTJE area. (C.27.d.36) Where one section is in reserve. The relief was completed by 5p.m. There was practically no shelling throughout the day. The Coy relieved the 227th H.A.C. in the Divisional reserve line on the Gravenstaffel Ridge. The O.C. Coy and two sections at the CAPITOL D14.d.0515 with sites for 4 emergency guns on ABRAHAM heights and 2 emergency guns on HILL 37. One Section with Section H'Qrs. at KOREK. 2 guns at D9.c.45 and two at D9.d.44. One Section with Section H'Qrs. at WURST FARM with 2 guns at D8.d.12 (BOETLEER) and two guns at D8.b.21. One Section at Rear H'Qrs. D. Camp WILTJE area C.27.b.61. The relief was completed by 4-30 p.m.	

WAR DIARY
or
INTELLIGENCE SUMMARY.

(Erase heading not required.)

Army Form C. 2118.

Place	Date	Hour	Summary of Events and Information	Remarks and references to Appendices
	Feb. 13th 1918		The Sector was fairly quiet except for intermittent shelling. Much time was spent in salvaging.	
	14th Feb		The usual hostile shelling was supplemented by gas shelling in the area between KOREK & WURST FARM.	
	15th Feb		Usual hostile shelling. An inter-Section relief took place.	
	16th Feb		One H.O.R.E. was admitted to hospital. The usual hostile artillery activity. Enemy prisoners were elected. Salvage work was carried on.	
	17th Feb		Construction of sleeping accommodation commenced at GALLIPOLI in pill boxes. Normal activity of enemy.	
	18th Feb		An inter-Section relief took place. No 9 Section coming up from Rear H.Qrs. and No 7 going out. Fairly quiet on Sector except for heavy counter-battery work.	
	19th Feb		Site for emergency guns at Hut 37 abandoned and new positions chosen at DOCHY FARM. Work was commenced here. A considerable amount of salvage was sent back to Battn. H.Qrs.	

Army Form C. 2118.

WAR DIARY
INTELLIGENCE SUMMARY.
(Erase heading not required.)

Place	Date	Hour	Summary of Events and Information	Remarks and references to Appendices
	20th Sept 1918		The new S.O.S. (2 Reds & 2 Greens) came into force today. Our Batteries were active. Weather hard and clear good observation. One of our aeroplanes came down in flames, both occupants killed.	
	21st		The usual hostile activity. An inter-section relief took place.	
	22nd		The enemy's artillery was active. A concentration of fire was carried out by enemy on the forward slope of the GRAVENSTAFEL ridge. The field of fire of the four guns at KOREK was altered. The two right guns had their zero lines on LAMKEEK with a traverse of 45° on either side. The two left guns were laid on PETER PAN with a similar angle of traverse.	
	23rd		Of the four guns at WURST FARM the two right guns were laid on KRON PRINZ F.M. with a 45° traverse on each side. Hostile activity was normal	
	24th		Four Gun positions were commenced in BERLIN WOOD to cover the RAVEBEEK. Valley and four Gun positions were commenced at KRON PRINZ F.M. The O.C. 29th M.G. Baltn visited the Gun positions. An inter-section relief took place.	

Army Form C. 2118.

WAR DIARY
or
INTELLIGENCE SUMMARY.
(Erase heading not required.)

Instructions regarding War Diaries and Intelligence Summaries are contained in F. S. Regs., Part II. and the Staff Manual respectively. Title pages will be prepared in manuscript.

Place	Date	Hour	Summary of Events and Information	Remarks and references to Appendices
	25th		Normal activity	
	26th		Work continued on positions at DOCHY F^m and KRONPRINZ F^m. 1. O.R wounded.	
	27th		Work continued. A further supply of Salvage sent down.	
	28th		Usual Programme pursued. Hostile activity normal.	

M. Johnston Lt.
for O.C. 11th Machine Gun Coy

ATTACHED
23RD DIVISION
24TH INFY BDE

24TH MACHINE GUN COY.
JAN - JUN 1916

War Diary of 24th Machine
Gun Company for months
of January, February, March
1916.

Jan '16
June '16

WAR DIARY of 24th Machine Gun Army Form C. 2118.
Company
or
INTELLIGENCE SUMMARY

(Erase heading not required.)

Instructions regarding War Diaries and Intelligence Summaries are contained in F. S. Regs., Part II. and the Staff Manual respectively. Title Pages will be prepared in manuscript.

Place	Date	Hour	Summary of Events and Information	Remarks and references to Appendices
B.26.A.7.6.	1916 Jan 24th Mon.		Company was formed. Detachments of 16 men 2 corporals two sergeants and 2 officers joined from each regiment. Lt Lewis in Command of Company during absence of Captain Porter on leave. Lt Constant from Worcestershire Regiment Lt Lewis & Lt Friend from 2nd E San Regt. Lt Perkins & Lt Fletcher from 1/Sherwood Foresters 2nd Lt Roydes & Boulter from 2nd Northampton Regt. C.S.M Wilson from 1st Sherwood Foresters. Q.M.S Humphreys from 1/Worcester Regt Company billeted at B26A 7 & 6 opposite JESUS Farm SW of ERQUINGHEM.	HP
"	Tues. 25th		Four limbers one mess cart and a water cart arrived from Div'l Train Also eleven horses 5 Drivers and Shoeing Smith Jr Jarvis	HP
"	Wed. 26th		Parades 7am Roll Call attended by Orderly Officer 7.30 - 8 Physical Training 8.0 am Breakfasts. 9.15 am Orderly Room 10.30 - 11.30 Parades - inspection etc. 12.45 Dinner 2 - 2.45 Parade 9pm Roll Call. The Inspections were held: Tube helmets, iron rations Field dressings etc	HP

2449 Wt. W14957/M90 750,000 1/16 J.B.C. & A. Forms/C.2118/12.

Army Form C. 2118.

WAR DIARY
or
INTELLIGENCE SUMMARY

(Erase heading not required.)

Instructions regarding War Diaries and Intelligence Summaries are contained in F. S. Regs., Part II. and the Staff Manual respectively. Title Pages will be prepared in manuscript.

Place	Date	Hour	Summary of Events and Information	Remarks and references to Appendices
B 2 6 A½ 6	Jan 26 Thurs.		Gun drill for No 1 Sect — renewing sections, fatigues clearing mud away from barn, and cleaning out small billet afterwards condemned by M.O.	AP
	Jan 27 Friday		Parades and Fatigues as usual. Horse lines commenced — Drivers of 8 Lan. Limber commenced laying bricks.	AP
	Jan 28th		Parades as usual etc.	AP
	Jan 29th Sunday		Nil. Fine day — cold. Church Parade (CE) 10.45 am. Lt Boulter left on leave	AP
	Jan 30th		Pro rain — very muddy. Lt Boulter's leave began officially. Bricklayer sent from 1/Sherwood Foresters.	AP
	Jan 31st		Fine day. 5-7 men under Lt Bougetel went to Gun Batts at ERQUINGHEM. No's 3 & 1 subsection of No 2 left for Trenches. The former went into line occupied by 1/Sherwood Foresters — the latter into line occupied by 2nd E Lancashire Regiment.	P

H C Porter Capt
OC 2lt
31/1/16

Army Form C. 2118.

WAR DIARY
or
INTELLIGENCE SUMMARY
(Erase heading not required.)

Place	Date	Hour	Summary of Events and Information	Remarks and references to Appendices
B26A 17:6	Feb 1st 1916		Capt Porter 60th Rifles joined company from leave and took over command of Company from Lt Lewis — very fine day	AF
"	2nd		Fine weather in morning clouded over later in day. One hut finished by R.E. for office & store	AF
"	3rd		Very fine day — Parades as usual.	
"	4th		Very strong wind from East & some rain. No 4 Section under 2nd Lt Pougett relieved 4 guns of the Motor Machine Gun Corps in the BOIS GRENIER line of trenches. No 1 Section under 2nd Lt Heurtault relieved No 3 Section & remains half section of No 2 Sect. relieved the other half of same section in front line trenches. No 3rd Subsection No 2 return to H.Q.	AF
"	5th		Very fine day. Limbered waggons used as ammunition carts exchanged for S.A.A. carts, one from each of following units 1/Worcesters 2/East Lan. 2nd Sherwood Foresters 1/Northamptons.	
"	6th		Fine day — parades as usual. 6 men from each of following units 2/Sherwoods 2/Eden & 7 men from each of following 1 Worcester, 1 Northampton joined R.E. Q'rs for temporary duty.	AF
"	7th		Much rain during night but fine during day. 2nd Lt Boulter rejoins from leave. Parades as usual.	AF
"	8th		Lt Boulter rejoins from leave. 2nd Lt Storman 1/Worcestershire Regt joins H.Q'rs from a machine gun course at WISQUES — Religion trenches carried out by No 3 Sec. Relieving No 1 & No 2 Sect. proving to run relief.	AF
"	9th		Parades as usual	AF
"	10th		Parades as usual	AF

Army Form C. 2118.

WAR DIARY
or
INTELLIGENCE SUMMARY

(Erase heading not required.)

Instructions regarding War Diaries and Intelligence Summaries are contained in F. S. Regs., Part II. and the Staff Manual respectively. Title Pages will be prepared in manuscript.

Place	Date	Hour	Summary of Events and Information	Remarks and references to Appendices
B26A:7:6	Feb. 11th		No 1 Sec. relieved No 3 in trenches & No 2 Section carries out its own relief — Everything normal	HP
"	12th		Heavy shelling by enemy along BOIS GRENIER Line & on roads behind — very cloudy day	HP
"	13th		Heavy shelling by enemy on BOIS GRENIER Line & roads as on previous day. RUE MARLE shelled also	HP
"	14th		The No 1 & No 2 machine guns relieved No 4 Section in BOIS GRENIER Line & MG of 103rd Inf Bde relieved No. 1 & 2 Sect in front line	HP
"	15th		Very windy day. 2 guns of No 3 Sect. & 2 guns of No 4 Sect sent to Hd Qrs No 2 Brigade at FLEURBAIX for temporary attachment — 1 man also per gun attached	HP
"	16th		Section Parade — everything normal	HP
"	17th		Section Parade "	HP
"	18th		Section Parade "	HP
"	19th		Section Parade "	HP
VIEUX BERQUIN	20th		24th Inf Brigade under orders to proceed to III Corps Reserve, marches via HOLLABREN & MENEGATE to VIEUX BERQUIN. Company arrives at VIEUX BERQUIN 5 pm and is billeted there for night. Very fine day. MG Company in rear of column.	HP
LABELLE HOTESSE	21st		24th Inf Brigade continues march at 8.30 am from VIEUX BERQUIN, MG Company being in rear of Column and arrives at LABELLE HOTESSE via LAMOTTE & STEENBECQUE about 1 pm. MG company takes up billets S/ of LA BELLE HOTESSE. Company HQrs being at I 3:B 5:4. Very fine day	HP
I 3B 5:4	22nd		Section parades and general cleaning up of billets — snows hard most of day.	HP
"	23rd		Orders received about 9 am that Bde is under orders to move to ESTAIRE next day — 2 am telephone message received to say this move is "postponed" — snowing and freezing most of day	HP

Army Form C. 2118.

WAR DIARY
or
INTELLIGENCE SUMMARY
(Erase heading not required.)

Place	Date	Hour	Summary of Events and Information	Remarks and references to Appendices
I 3 B 5.7	24th Feb.		Freezing and thawing	MR
"	25th		About 3" snow on ground — Company route march	MR
"	26th		A rapid thaw set in in afternoon. Company exercised on 25st Range. Brigade becomes in GHQ Reserve	MR
"	27th		Thaw continues	MR
"	28th		Orders received for 24th R.G. Company to to move to BRUAY on morning of 29th. Transport by road, men by train.	MR
"	29th		Transport moved from billets at LABELLE HOTESSE to billets in BRUAY arriving at THIENNES & proceeded by train to Company entered at THIENNES & proceeded by train to latter place about 3pm — the company entered by road under Lieut. CALONNE RICQUART; thence by march. Transport moved by road under Lieut. Lewis their route being via MORBECQUE, STVENANT–LILLERS–BRUAY. Good billets	MR

Henderson Capt
O.C. 24 R.G. Company
29/2/16

WAR DIARY or INTELLIGENCE SUMMARY

Army Form C. 2118.

(Erase heading not required.)

Place	Date	Hour	Summary of Events and Information	Remarks and references to Appendices
BRUAY	March 1st		Snowed Heavily. however men comfortable in billets	HR
"	2nd		More snow. The 24th Inf Brigade including 24th MG Company was inspected by the IV Corps Commander outside HQ of 24th Inf Bde at 9.30 a.m. Company's heavy baggage from LA BELLE HOTESSE arrives at BRUAY by motor lorry.	HR
"	3rd		Snows hard	HR
"	4th		OC MG Company proceeds to ABLAIN St NAZAIRE to reconnoitre ground on NOTRE DAME de LORETTE to be taken over on 6th by 1st Bn Sherwood Foresters at 4 guns of No 3 Sect. MG Company. Snows hard. The French in occupation of these lines are obliging but not Helpful.	HR
"	5th		No 3 Section under Lieut Perkins proceed to billets in GRAND SERVINS, preparatory to taking over position at NOTRE DAME de LORETTE from French	HR
"	6th		More snow - orders received for 24th Inf Bde to move from BRUAY to SERVINS area to take over CARENCY section of trench from French. No 3 Section takes over trenches on N. Dame de LORETTE from French	HR
GRAND SERVINS	7th		24th Inf Bde less 1 Bn Sherwood Foresters & No 3 sectn. MG Company move by route march to SERVINS area arriving there about noon - very fine day. Machine Gun Company is billeted in GRAND SERVINS.	HR
"	8th		More snow - V. cold - four billets. All transport horses are put under cover.	HR

WAR DIARY
or
INTELLIGENCE SUMMARY

Army Form C. 2118.

(Erase heading not required.)

Instructions regarding War Diaries and Intelligence Summaries are contained in F. S. Regs., Part II. and the Staff Manual respectively. Title Pages will be prepared in manuscript.

Place	Date	Hour	Summary of Events and Information	Remarks and references to Appendices
BRUAY GRAND SERVIN	9th March		Snow 4" thick on ground.	AP
"		10:15	O C Company reconnoitres positions of machine guns on two right sections of 69th Bde front trenches preparatory to taking over these trenches from 69th Bde Bde. It is impossible to get into left section of Bde trenches as these can only be got into under cover of night	AP
"		11:15	24th M G Company takes over positions in front line trenches CARENCY section from 69th M G Company - having 14 guns in front line & 2 guns at CARENCY village in Reserve. No 1 & 2 sections on right & centre sections. No 3 & 4 sections on No 1 & 2 sections on right with remaining 1/2 No 3 section proceeding left section. Sergeant Jack with remaining 1/2 No 3 Company. to CARENCY in Reserve on relief by 69th M G Company. trenches the 69th M G Company hand over to 24th M G Company on 24th M G 14 Vickers guns & ammunition &c to replace these the 24th M G Company. hand over complete with ammunition spare parts etc 13 Maxim guns & 1 Vickers gun to 69 M G Company Deep snow on ground otherwise fine though misty. Transport stops at GRAND SERVIN. O C Company with 24th July Bde Hqrs at ABLAIN ST NAZAIRE	AP

Army Form C. 2118.

WAR DIARY
or
INTELLIGENCE SUMMARY

(Erase heading not required.)

Instructions regarding War Diaries and Intelligence Summaries are contained in F.S. Regs., Part II. and the Staff Manual respectively. Title Pages will be prepared in manuscript.

Place	Date	Hour	Summary of Events and Information	Remarks and references to Appendices
ABLAIN ST NAZAIRE	March 12th		Trenches taken over. Ground was very bad and wet. No suitable places for machine guns or dug outs for the teams. 2 guns in left section withdrawn from front line and placed in Reserve in "QUARRIES". L/c Richou No.1 Section killed by sniper.	AP
"	March 13		Quiet day in trenches with exception of activity by enemy's aerial torpedoes. 2nd Lt Rougelet reports sick. 2" trench guns of OC Company sent to plot gun	AP
"	March 14		2nd Lt Rougelet returns to MG Company Store Room at GRAND SERVINS where he remains. OC Company sent to plot gun positions in a Reserve line at BOYEFFLES. Rapid thaw, warm & bright	AP
"	March 15		24th R.G Company is relieved by 141st M.G Company & march back to GRAND SERVINS bringing guns etc with them. Except for much activity by enemy aerial torpedoes this tour in trenches has been quiet. The relief of 24th M G Coy is delayed about 2 hours by enemy shelling CARENCY. Company complete in billets at GRAND SERVINS about 2.30 a.m. Very fine day	AP

Army Form C. 2118.

WAR DIARY
or
INTELLIGENCE SUMMARY

(Erase heading not required.)

Instructions regarding War Diaries and Intelligence Summaries are contained in F. S. Regs., Part II and the Staff Manual respectively. Title Pages will be prepared in manuscript.

Place	Date	Hour	Summary of Events and Information	Remarks and references to Appendices
GRAND SERVINS	March 16		Company moves to OURTON Chateau to Reserve Billets – arriving there about 4 pm	KD
OURTON	March 17th		General Clean up – company to paid out – Orders received to re-exchange guns with 69th M G Company at BRUAY.	KD
"	"	18th	Inspection of 69th M G Company by O C 24th M G Company – Satisfactory. Guns taken over to 69th M G Company and exchanged with guns & ammunition belonging to 24th M G Company in presence of former O C Company V.J.	KD
"	"	19th	Stay C in C rides round billets at OURTON. Fine day. O C Company reconnoitres new trenches to be taken over from 99th M G Coy. During this AIX NOULETTE heavily shelled. Lt Rougetel reports back & is transferred to England	KD
"	"	20	Company moves from OURTON to billets at HERSIN – starting 1 pm & arriving about 5 pm. No 1 & 4 Sections under 2/Lt Courtauld & Boutflour respectively proceed further to AIX-NOULETTE preparatory to taking over trenches 21st inst.	KD

Army Form C. 2118.

WAR DIARY
or
INTELLIGENCE SUMMARY

(Erase heading not required.)

Instructions regarding War Diaries and Intelligence Summaries are contained in F. S. Regs., Part II. and the Staff Manual respectively. Title Pages will be prepared in manuscript.

Place	Date	Hour	Summary of Events and Information	Remarks and references to Appendices
HERSIN	March 21		No 1 & 4 Sections take over B gun positions & front line system from 99th Bde. Remainder of Company takeover Billets from 99th Bde at AIX NOULETTE & transport lines at BOUVIGNY. 2 Lt Fletcher & 4 men who had been at M G School at WISQUES rejoin the Company. Fine day	AP
AIX NOULETTE	22		Fine day — O.C. Company visits gun in front system of SOUCHEZ 70K. Fry right, quiet in trenches.	AP
"	23		Fine day — quiet in trenches — snow at night	AP
"	24th		Fine day — good deal of shelling in front line trenches in SOUCHEZ I. Shells falling close to gun of No 1 Section, but no casualties. Leave is reopened.	AP
	25		No 2 & 3 Sections relieve No 1 & 4 Section in trenches respectively. Taking over guns & ammunition stores & handing over guns & ammunition to billets. Relief complete 11 p.m. Lieut Lewis the 2 O.R. proceed on 7days leave to England.	AP
	26		Friday but heavy rain at night — No 1 & 4 Sections bath at Brigade bath in AIX - NOULETTE	AP

Army Form C. 2118.

WAR DIARY
or
INTELLIGENCE SUMMARY
(Erase heading not required.)

Place	Date	Hour	Summary of Events and Information	Remarks and references to Appendices
AIX NOULETTE	March 27		OC Company reconnoitres ground on northern spurs of NOTRE DAME de LORETTE in "BAJOLLE" & MAISTRE lines for positions for MG. Very fine day.	
"	28		Quiet in Trenches & everything normal.	
"	29		All quiet & normal - 3. OR proceed on 7 days leave to England. No 1&4 Sections in billets where No 2 & 3 Sections in trenches - no casualties.	
"	30	30	All Ranks MG Company attend a Flammenwerfer demonstration at SAINS EN GOHELLE - very reassuring exhibition. AIX NOULETTE & Company billets shelled fairly continuously during morning by 4.2 Shells. Great aerial enemy activity.	
"	31		Fine day. No 2 & 3 Sections bath at Brigade baths AIX NOULETTE Good deal of shelling of company's billets about 7 am - no casualties. Good deal of machine gun fire at night in trenches.	

JCMPorter Captain
OC 24th mg Company

31/3/16

Vol IV

WAR DIARY
of
24th Inf Bde MACHINE Gun Company for Month of April 1916

Army Form C. 2118.

24th Machine Gun Company WAR DIARY for Month of April 1916

INTELLIGENCE SUMMARY

Place	Date	Hour	Summary of Events and Information	Remarks and references to Appendices
AIX-NOULETTE	Ap 1	—	The Company has 8 guns in front line system of SOUCHEZ I & II & 8 guns & gun teams in billets in AIX NOULETTE. Transport lines being at BOUVIGNY. & Company HQrs at AIX NOULETTE. No 1 & 4 Sections are in Trenches.	AP
"	Ap 2nd		Everything quiet & normal. Obs	AP
"	Ap 3rd		Everything normal — Fine weather. No 2 & 3 Sections relieve No Sections in trenches. Company paid out by sections — Lt Gorman and 10R proceed by bus from Bde HQrs on leave (7days) to England	AP
"	Ap 4th		Everything normal. Fine weather. Parades in billets as usual	AP
"	Ap 5th		All quiet and normal.	AP
"	Ap 6th		No 1 & 4 Sections relieve No 2 & 3 Sections in Trenches	AP

WAR DIARY
or
INTELLIGENCE SUMMARY

Army Form C. 2118.

(Erase heading not required.)

Place	Date	Hour	Summary of Events and Information	Remarks and references to Appendices
AIX NOULETTE	Ap 7th		All quiet & normal - fine warm weather.	HR
"	Ap 8th		" "	HR
"	Ap 9th		Good deal of activity in SOUCHEZ I from enemy 5.9 shells & aerial torpedoes. Pte Plumb No 4 Section (temporarily attached to No 1 Section) killed & 2 O.R. wounded - (an aerial torpedo in front line trench SOUCHEZ I.	HR
"	Ap 10th		All quiet & normal. Artillery & smoke demonstration by our division & 47th Div Sien, not particularly successful so far as one could judge, since it resulted in no retaliation on enemy's part. Weather warm, no wind.	HR
"	Ap 11th		All quiet and normal - No 2 & 3 Sections relieve 104 Sections in trenches. Wet day. Pte Plumb buried at AIX NOULETTE Cemetery.	HR
"	Ap 12th		Wet cold day, everything normal.	HR
"	Ap 13th		" " All leave stopped.	HR

Army Form C. 2118.

WAR DIARY
or
INTELLIGENCE SUMMARY

(Erase heading not required.)

Instructions regarding War Diaries and Intelligence Summaries are contained in F. S. Regs., Part II. and the Staff Manual respectively. Title Pages will be prepared in manuscript.

Place	Date	Hour	Summary of Events and Information	Remarks and references to Appendices
April 14 – Aix NOULETTE	Ap 14		All quiet & normal in Trenches & at AIX NOULETTE – but BOUVIGNY Wood Transport lines are is shelled by a few 5.9 shells presumably ranging	AP
"	Ap 15		All quiet & normal in Trenches, but BOUVIGNY shelled again – 3 limbers being hit, 2 of which belonging to No 3 Section became unehrs & have to be sent into ordnance to be repaired. Transport lines are moved to BOUEFFLES.	AP
"	Ap 16		No 2 & 3 Sections are relieved in Trenches by guns of 99th Inf Bde & return to AIX NOULETTE – very wet night & some activity on right of our trench line during night by 4 & 7th Div. Relief completed however without casualties.	AP
"	Ap 17		2 & 4 M.G. Company having been relieved by 99th Bde moves to HERSIN to billets there for night – arrive in billets there about 10 pm. Fine night but very heavy showers during day.	AP
HERSIN. Ap 18	Ap 18		Company moves from HERSIN to billets in BRUAY in the "rest area", arriving there by route march about 3pm. Fine day. Fair billets.	AP

WAR DIARY
or
INTELLIGENCE SUMMARY

Army Form C. 2118.

(Erase heading not required.)

Place	Date	Hour	Summary of Events and Information	Remarks and references to Appendices
BRUAY	Ap 19th		Fine day - General Clean up of billets which are very dirty & insanitary -	AP
"	Ap 20th		Parades as usual.	AP
"	Ap 21st		Good Friday. Church Parade for R. Catholics, but no services for other denominations	AP
"	Ap 22nd		Parades as usual, but very wet indeed & impossible to do much.	AP
"	Ap 23		Easter Day. C of E Parade Service near Billets at 9.20.	AP
"	Ap 24		Parades as usual. Commanding Officers Conference at Bde HQrs.	AP
"	Ap 25		Company moved from BRUAY by route march to SAINS- LES- PERNES to billets there for night - very hot day - arrive in billets about 6am. Before leaving BRUAY the company no inspected by Doctor attached to East Lan: Regiment. 3 men admitted Hosp, suffering from Scabies.	B

Army Form C. 2118.

WAR DIARY
or
INTELLIGENCE SUMMARY

(Erase heading not required.)

Instructions regarding War Diaries and Intelligence Summaries are contained in F. S. Regs., Part II. and the Staff Manual respectively. Title Pages will be prepared in manuscript.

Place	Date	Hour	Summary of Events and Information	Remarks and references to Appendices
SAINS-LES-PERNES	Ap 26		Company moves from SAINS-LES-PERNES by route march to billets in the IV Corp manoeuvre area at VINCLY. Starting 8.30 a.m. & arriving VINCLY about 1.30 p.m. Very hot day. Good billets at VINCLY. Leave having reopened 2 O.R. proceed on leave.	P.
VINCLY	Ap 27		Range practice for all four sections. Very fine & V. hot	R
"	Ap 28		Company Tactical Exercise. V. hot.	R
"	Ap 29		Company exercised in digging. Hasty emplacements etc. V. hot.	R
"	Ap 30		Company on ranges (400 x 25t) - also taught how to throw Mills bombs - 144 live bombs being thrown. V. hot	R.

H.C.M. Porter Captain
OC 24th Inf Bde Machine Gun Company
30/4/16

War Diary
of
24th Brigade Machine
Gun Company
for Month of
May 1916.

Army Form C. 2118.

WAR DIARY
24th Infantry Brigade Machine Gun Company
INTELLIGENCE SUMMARY

(Erase heading not required.)

Place	Date	Hour	Summary of Events and Information	Remarks and references to Appendices
VINCLY	May 1st		Company still in billets at VINCLEY in the manoeuvre area of IVCorps. Very hot — back in billets about 3p.m. Brigade Field day. 2 OR proceed on leave to England.	
VINCLY	May 2nd		The Company had received orders to move to PALFART to billet there for night starting 2.45pm. But these orders cancelled 4pm & Company received orders to remain at VINCLEY & own O.R.S. stay instead — Heavy thunderstorms.	
"	May 3rd		Shooting on range for all sections & classes. Sergeant Horbick No 1 Sect awarded Military Medal for gallantry in trenches SOUCHEZ I on Ap 9th 1916	
"	May 4		The Company moves to PALFART to billet there for night en route for HERSIN.	

Army Form C. 2118.

WAR DIARY
or
INTELLIGENCE SUMMARY
(Erase heading not required.)

Instructions regarding War Diaries and Intelligence Summaries are contained in F. S. Regs., Part II and the Staff Manual respectively. Title Pages will be prepared in manuscript.

Place	Date	Hour	Summary of Events and Information	Remarks and references to Appendices
PALFART	May 5		Company moves to billets in HERSIN. Transport by road, men & Company entrain at PERNES to BARLIN thence by road.	AP
HERSIN	May 6		Parades as usual	AP
"	7th		Church Parade at 9 a.m.	AP
"	8th		Inspection of Company by O.C. 23rd Div: en Transport lines	AP
"	9th		No's 1 & 4 Sections relieve 2 Sections of 99th M.G. Co. in SOUCHEZ Left. These sections move off from HERSIN at 7 p.m. — relief complete 12.15 a.m. Very wet night	AP
HERSIN	10		Head Quarters & 2 & 3 Sect. move to billets in AIX NOULETTE Transport to BOUETTLES.	AP

2449 Wt. W14957/M90 750,000 1/16 J.B.C. & A. Forms/C.2118/12.

Army Form C. 2118.

WAR DIARY
or
INTELLIGENCE SUMMARY

(Erase heading not required.)

Instructions regarding War Diaries and Intelligence Summaries are contained in F. S. Regs., Part II. and the Staff Manual respectively. Title Pages will be prepared in manuscript.

Place	Date	Hour	Summary of Events and Information	Remarks and references to Appendices
AIX NOULETTE	May 11th		No's 1 & 4 Sections in SOUCHEZ I & II - Everything normal	R.
	12th		"	
	13th		"	
	14th		"	
	15th		"	
	16th		No's 2 & 3 Sections take over 8 gun positions from 141st In J Company on NOTRE DAME de LORETTE. No 1 & 4 Sections (after having been relieved by 2 sections of 68th J.Co.) SP & HdQrs & Transport of Company move in SOUCHEZ I & II) and HdQrs & Transport of Company move to billets in huts in BOIS VIGNY wood, arriving there about 12 m.n.	

WAR DIARY or INTELLIGENCE SUMMARY

Army Form C. 2118.

Place	Date	Hour	Summary of Events and Information	Remarks and references to Appendices
BOUVIGNY WOOD	17th May		Everything normal & quiet. weather very fine.	SR
	18th May		"	
	19th May		"	
	20th May		No 2 & 3 Sections still on NOTRE DAME de LORETTE, but remainder of Company & transport move from BOUVIGNY wood to billets in BOUVIGNY, arriving there about 9 p.m. Very fine.	SR
	21st May		Heavy bombardment by tear shells on N D de LORETTE & BOUVIGNY woods synchronises with hurricane fire by enemy in trenches held by 47th Divn on VIMY Ridge about 3 p.m – 5 p.m. The enemy take trenches from 47th Divn; 2nd Lt Company "stands to". expecting orders to move, but none come. OC Company goes on leave for 10 days to ENGLAND also Lt Courtauld.	

Army Form C. 2118.

WAR DIARY
or
INTELLIGENCE SUMMARY
(Erase heading not required.)

Instructions regarding War Diaries and Intelligence Summaries are contained in F. S. Regs., Part II. and the Staff Manual respectively. Title Pages will be prepared in manuscript.

Place	Date	Hour	Summary of Events and Information	Remarks and references to Appendices
BOUVIGNY.	May 22nd		Very heavy & continuous shelling on VIMY Ridge – Company ordered to "stand to" at 9 pm. but nothing followed.	AR
"	23rd		Very heavy shelling on VIMY Continues – Company ordered to be ready to move at a moments notice about 8pm, but nothing happens.	AR
"	24th		No 1 & 4 Sect. relieve No 2 & 3 Section on N DAME de LORETTE.	AR
"	25th		Everything normal on N DAME & round BOUVIGNY.	AR
"	26		"	"
"	27		"	"
"	28th		No 2 & 3 Section relieve 2 Section of 69th M.g Company in ANGRES Sector; No 1 Section is relieved in N Dame by 1 sect of 69th R. g Company	AR

2449 Wt. W14957/M90 750,000 1/16 J.B.C. & A. Forms/C.2118/12.

WAR DIARY
or
INTELLIGENCE SUMMARY

(Erase heading not required.)

Army Form C. 2118.

Place	Date	Hour	Summary of Events and Information	Remarks and references to Appendices
BOUVIGNY	May 29th		No 1 Sect. takes over portion in ANGRES Sector from 1 Sect of 69th In. Company - No 4 Sect in N DAME is relieved by 1 Sect 69th In. g Company.	App
BOUVIGNY	May 30th		Company H'd Qrs & No 4 Sect move from BOUVIGNY to billets in Transport Lines in BOIS de FROISSART. FOSSE. 10.	App
FOSSE 10	May 31st		Everything Normal - FOSSE 10 shelled by enemy	App

H.C.M Porter Major
OC 24th In. g Company

War Diary
of
24th Bde Machine Gun Company.
for
June 1916

Army Form C. 2118.

WAR DIARY 224 M.G. Company
or
INTELLIGENCE SUMMARY 23rd Div.

(Erase heading not required.)

Place	Date	Hour	Summary of Events and Information	Remarks and references to Appendices
FOSSE 10	June 1st		Company Hd Qrs & No 4 Sect. at FOSSE 10, Transport lines in BOIS de PROISSART, No 1, 2 & 3 Sections in ANGRES TAIL, all Quiet & normal.	AP
"	June 2nd		S.O.S Barrage received from SOCHEZ II about 7.15 pm. Company "stood to" but nothing follows. O.C. Company & Lt Courtauld return from leave	AP
"	3rd		Fosse 10 - shelled by enemy chiefly around Minehead	AP
"	4th		All quiet & normal.	AP
"	5th	"		AP
"	6th	"	Pte A Cult awarded D.C.M, & Pte Leslie the Military Medal for actions previous to joining the company.	AP

Army Form C. 2118.

WAR DIARY
or
INTELLIGENCE SUMMARY
(Erase heading not required.)

Instructions regarding War Diaries and Intelligence Summaries are contained in F.S. Regs., Part II. and the Staff Manual respectively. Title Pages will be prepared in manuscript.

Place	Date	Hour	Summary of Events and Information	Remarks and references to Appendices
FOSSE 10	JUNE 7th		No 2 Section relieves No 3 Section which returns to FOSSE 10.	
	8th		All quiet & normal	
	9th		" " "	
	10th		" " "	
	11th		" " "	
	12th		Sections in trenches relieved by 141st M.G. Company	
	13th		Company moves to PRESSY-LES-PERNES en route for manoeuvre area. Starting 7.30 AM.	
	14th		Move continued to FIEFS starting 8.30 AM.	
	15th		G.O.C. M.G. corps inspection ordered but cancelled.	
PRESSY-LES-PERNES	16th		Company leave FIEFS 9.30AM & arrive Company Groueppe 11AM	

WAR DIARY or INTELLIGENCE SUMMARY

Army Form C. 2118.

Place	Date	Hour	Summary of Events and Information	Remarks and references to Appendices
GROEUPPE	JUNE 17th		Inspection by G.O.C. Machine Gun corps. near BEAUMETZ-LES-AIRES.	
	18th		Church parade 8.30 AM. All Sections carried out firing practice on manoeuvre area during morning.	
	19th		Company marched to FLECHINELLE for baths arriving back at 2.30 PM.	
	20th		Company engaged in open order & advanced Co drill on manoeuvre area.	
	21st		Same as 20th.	
	22nd		Same as 20th.	
	23rd		Inspection parade in morning. Transport move 10.45 PM. to LILLERS Station.	
	24th		Company less Transport leave 1.30 A.M for LILLERS Station. Entire company arrive LONGEAU 3.45 PM. & march to billets at S.t SAVEUR 8.30 PM.	

Army Form C. 2118.

WAR DIARY
or
INTELLIGENCE SUMMARY

(Erase heading not required.)

Instructions regarding War Diaries and Intelligence Summaries are contained in F. S. Regs., Part II. and the Staff Manual respectively. Title Pages will be prepared in manuscript.

Place	Date	Hour	Summary of Events and Information	Remarks and references to Appendices
ST. SAUVEUR	June 25		Cleaning up parades	
	26		Company engaged on limber drill by sections.	
	27		Wet day Sections parade in billets for instruction in mechanism.	
	28		Order to move received in morning but cancelled in afternoon	
	29		Company engaged by sections in morning on route march in morning.	
	30		Company parade in morning for Signalling practice Move to RAINNEVILLE in afternoon.	

J.B.C. Muir Capt.
O.C. 24th Bde. M.G.C.

1.7.16

www.ingramcontent.com/pod-product-compliance
Lightning Source LLC
Chambersburg PA
CBHW082008220426
43670CB00014B/2582